Europe

Europe

The Faltering Project

JÜRGEN HABERMAS

Translated by
CIARAN CRONIN

polity

First published in German as *Ach, Europa* © Suhrkamp Verlag Frankfurt am Main, 2008

This English edition differs in some respects from the original German text. Several pieces have been removed and three new pieces have been added: 'What is Meant by a "Post-secular Society?"', 'The Constitutionalization of International Law and the Problems of Legitimating a Constitution for World Society', and the Afterword, 'Lessons of the Financial Crisis'.

Polity Press
65 Bridge Street
Cambridge CB2 1UR, UK.

Polity Press
350 Main Street
Malden, MA 02148, USA

'The translation of this work was supported by a grant from the Goethe-Institut which is funded by the German Ministry of Foreign Affairs.'

ISBN-13: 978-0-7456-4640-4
ISBN-13: 978-0-7456-4649-7(pb)

A catalogue record for this book is available from the British Library.

Typeset in 11 on 13 pt Berling
by SNP Best-set Typesetter Ltd, Hong Kong
Printed and bound in Great Britain by MPG Books Group Ltd

The publisher has used its best endeavours to ensure that the URLs for external websites referred to in this book are correct and active at the time of going to press. However, the publisher has no responsibility for the websites and can make no guarantee that a site will remain live or that the content is or will remain appropriate.

For further information on Polity, visit our website: www.politybooks.com

Table of Contents

Author's Preface

Today all that remains of Enzensberger's eulogy to European diversity – *Europe, Europe!* – is the sighing tone. A discussion with the German foreign minister Frank-Walter Steinmeier provided me with an occasion for further reflection on the future of Europe and for trying to dispel the self-delusion that the danger of the European Union regressing into the all-too-familiar power games of the national governments has been banished by the Lisbon Summit. The course of European unification has been determined until now by the governments. But they now seem to be at their wits' end. Perhaps it is time for them to hand over responsibility for the future destiny of Europe to their peoples. Besides, I make a plea for a 'bipolar' unity of the West. I supplement the main topic with some occasional 'philosophical–political profiles' and with two texts on the role of the public sphere. The final essay is particularly close to my heart. It deals with the structuring influence that a normative theory of the public sphere can have on the design of empirical research.[1] Specialist journals have their problems with this topic because the social sciences and philosophy have drifted further apart than the founders of critical theory could ever have imagined.

Jürgen Habermas
Starnberg, November 2007

[1] See my commentary on this in *Acta Politica* 40/3 (2005): 384–92.

Translator's Preface

In the interview which concludes this volume, which was conducted as it was on the eve of the recent US presidential election and against the background of a mounting global financial crisis, Jürgen Habermas takes stock of the disastrous consequences of the decades-long dominance of neoliberal economic policy and of the neoconservative radicalization of US foreign policy under the Bush administration. Among the things that set his voice apart from the rising chorus of criticisms of neoliberalism and neoconservatism is his resolutely forward-looking perspective, remarkable in a thinker entering his ninth decade, and the analytic framework he brings to bear on these developments. Perhaps the most important issue these developments pose for him is whether the likely waning of US global dominance will herald a return to major power rivalry in international relations, as the so-called realists would have it, or whether it will prompt moves towards realizing the form of 'global governance without a world government' which he advocates. It may come as a surprise to some readers that Habermas attaches so much importance to another crisis – namely the constitutional crisis of the European Union and the stalling of the process of European unification – in deciding which of these competing models of global political governance may prevail in the coming decades. Habermas's theoretical engagement with the project of European integration features more or less centrally in most of the essays collected in this volume. But why, one may ask, does he attach so much global political importance to this seemingly provincial concern?

Habermas's writings on European issues must be understood against the background of his cosmopolitan model of global governance, which he contrasts with the realist vision of international relations. Realists argue that international relations are fundamentally anarchic and that a stable international order can be achieved only through a balance of power based on voluntary treaties between sovereign states. Habermas's contrasting model, which is inspired in part by Kant's cosmopolitanism, is predicated on the assumption that the individual and political basic rights on which democratic constitutions are founded also apply in principle to relations between states, organizations, and individuals across national borders. Thus for him the key issue in pacifying international relations concerns the form in which the institutions and procedures of political legitimation familiar from constitutional democracies can be extended to governance above the national level. Although this question remained moot during the post-war period of superpower rivalry, since 1989 at the latest – and since the acceleration in processes of globalization across different dimensions of world society – the need for new forms of political regulation above the national level has become increasingly apparent. The current financial crisis provides compelling evidence, if such is needed, that economic globalization poses political challenges which can be met only through concerted responses by the international community. Globalized markets have so far outstripped the regulatory competences of even the most powerful governments, and of existing regional and global economic regimes, that inclusive and representative global political institutions provide the only hope of bringing the rampant anarchy under control.

Habermas's proposed model of a future global political order (of which he provides an exposition and defense in Chapter 7) differs from more idealistic forms of cosmopolitanism in rejecting the goal of a world government that would supersede existing democratic nation–states. A world government is not viable because no single regime could possibly master the complexity of the matters in need of regulation – not to mention the problems raised by the diversity of languages, cultures, religions, and traditions within world society. It is not a normatively desirable goal either, because existing nation–states (or, at any rate those with more or less democratic constitutions) have a prima facie claim to continuing to exist as the legitimate representatives of their populations (and as the expressions of their national histories, traditions, and cultures). Thus a viable global political order will have to comprise at least two levels: the *national* level of the existing legitimate nation–states and of their populations; and the *supranational* level of a world organization tasked with enforcing human rights throughout the world. The nation–states would remain primarily responsible for securing the human rights and the well-being of their populations; they would retain their monopoly on the legitimate use of violence and would supply the world organization with the means of coercion it required in order to prevent or punish violations of human rights. This arrangement would restrict state sovereignty to the extent that government officials would no longer enjoy immunity from prosecution, and the right to go to war in pursuit of national interests would be abolished.

To these two levels of global governance would have to be added a third, *transnational* level, concerned with regulating matters of collective concern such as global economic crises and climate change, and based on inclusive negotiations and fair compromises among all concerned (including governments and regional and international organizations). In contrast to the 'thin' regime of human rights implementation at the supranational level, recourse to military power and criminal prosecution could play no role at the transnational level, so that agreement upon, and compliance with, regulatory regimes would have to be secured through compromises which are sensitive to conflicts of interests and imbalances of power in a global society. Thus Habermas refers to the 'thick' regulatory regimes which he envisages at the transnational level as the 'global domestic policy' of an emerging world society.

Realists will, of course, object that such a model is simply unrealistic (in the colloquial sense) or utopian. For why should a superpower like the United States accept the associated constraints on its scope for action (for instance in military matters) and make the necessary compromises in the pursuit of its national interests? Faced with this kind of objection, it is important to recognize that, even though the model involves certain unavoidable abstractions and idealizations, it is by no means simply an ideal opposed to existing international political realities. On the contrary, it represents an attempt to think through to their logical conclusion developments in the system of international institutions since the end of the nineteenth century and in international law since the end of the Second World War. To take the latter, since the Nuremberg and Tokyo War Trials and the 1949 UN Declaration of Human Rights, human rights principles have become ever more deeply anchored in international law and have assumed concrete institutional form in the United Nations. Indeed a possible route to the kind of supranational regime based on human rights which Habermas advocates would be through a reform of the United Nations in which the General Assembly would assume the role of a lower house, composed of representatives of the world's populations, and the Security Council would become an executive organ which would include representatives of all the member governments and would no longer be subject to the vetoes of a handful of powerful members. Thus the requisite project of reform can be described as a 'constitutionalization of international law', because it would involve developing existing principles of international law into a 'thin' constitution for the emerging world society.

It becomes clear against this background why the European project possesses both exemplary and strategic significance for Habermas. For if we consider where, under current conditions, the inspiration and concrete impulses for realizing such a global political order might come from, one likely answer is the European Union. The emerging major powers, such as China, India, Russia, and Brazil, are likely to be too preoccupied with the socially and environmentally disruptive consequences of explosive economic growth (and its inevitable cyclical downturns) to play a leading role in constructing a new global order. The most likely candidate to assume a leading role is the United States, for it will remain the most influential global power for the foreseeable future and it is in its own interest to bind these emerging powers into a more consensual global political order before they are in a position to challenge its superpower status. However, as Habermas argues, the United States – even under an enlightened President Obama, who manages to restore some of the respect and influence squandered by the Bush administration – cannot be expected to take the necessary initiatives without the material and moral support of its European ally. For President Obama is himself facing the daunting challenges of a domestic economic downturn and of extricating the United States from its military involvements in Iraq and Afghanistan without further destabilizing the region. And now that the neoconservative project of unilateral hegemony has been discredited, there is likely to be a resurgence of realist ideology among the Washington elites. For realism has deep historical roots in US political culture reaching back to the Monroe Doctrine.

Moreover, the development of the European Union from a treaty-based international alliance for economic cooperation into a body exercising extensive legislative, judicial, and administrative functions and including most

European countries can be seen as a regional exemplifica-
tion (though an incomplete and imperfect one) of the
model of global governance outlined. The EU has the
potential to serve as a model for regional regimes in other
parts of the world and as a catalyst for developments
toward a new global order – provided that the process of
political integration continues. A major problem, though,
is that the recent eastward expansion of the EU has
stretched the regulatory capacities of its institutions to
breaking point and has aggravated a constitutional crisis
which is threatening to derail political integration before
it has been accomplished. The European Constitution
(which was adopted by the member states, subject to
ratification, in 2004) was supposed to address the problem
of the 'democratic deficit' of the EU – namely the un-
representativeness and remoteness of its most powerful
institutions and the relative weakness of its only directly
elected body, the European Parliament – while making
possible the institutional reforms needed to cope with the
increased regulatory burdens of a body which has grown
to include twenty-seven member states. However, the
constitutional process was put on hold indefinitely by the
failure of the French and Dutch voters to ratify the constitution in 2005. In response to this debacle, the Lisbon
Treaty, which is subject to less stringent ratification
requirements, was adopted in 2007, in an effort to streamline the EU institutions and thus to make the enlarged
Union more governable. However, as Habermas argues, it
merely cements the existing status quo and thus in effect
stymies the constitutional process – and even its fate is
currently in the balance following the failure of Ireland to
ratify it in a referendum in June 2008.

For Habermas, one of the most serious consequences of
the internal divisions is the EU's relative lack of global
political influence, for want of a joint foreign and security
policy which would enable it to respond in coherent ways
to security and economy challenges. For example, because
the member states tend to operate as individual countries

pursuing their own national interests even in the context of joint military operations (whether under the aegis of the UN or of NATO), the EU was not able provide an effective counterweight to the United States when the latter was bent on invading Iraq, in violation of international law. Moreover, the incoherent response of the leading European economic powers to the current financial crisis seems to confirm a fatal tendency to fall back into the old patterns of nation-state rivalries.

The constitutional crisis reflects the deep ideological division within the EU between so-called Eurosceptics, who regard the EU primarily as a zone of economic cooperation and think that the lack of deeper political integration presents no obstacle to further enlargement, and federalists, who make the deepening of the political union a precondition for any further enlargement. This division mirrors the broader theoretical conflict between realists and those who think that the basic principles of constitutional democracy should also be implemented beyond the national level. Thus the fate of the process of European integration can be seen as a kind of 'crucial experiment' for Habermas's project of the constitutionalization of international law. In the light of this ideological cleavage, Habermas argues in Chapter 6 that the only way out of the current European dilemma is to continue the process of political integration at different speeds, with the EU adopting a policy of 'graduated integration'. This would enable the core of integrationist states, under the leadership of the founding members France, Germany, and Italy, to pursue a deeper political union by adopting a joint constitution, whereas the countries in the Eurosceptic camp – primarily Great Britain and the Scandinavian countries – could opt out for the present but would be free to join the integrationist core at any time in the future.

Among the theoretical issues at stake in controversies over the future of the EU and of the global political order, one which receives extensive treatment in this volume is that of the role of public reason as a source of democratic legitimation (see, in particular, Chapters 4, 8, and 9, and the discussions of three exemplary public intellectuals in the opening essays). Habermas defends a deliberative model of democracy which seeks to integrate the central insights of the dominant liberal and republican traditions – namely their focus on individual rights and on a shared national ethos respectively – within a communicative model of democratic legitimation. One of its distinctive features is the central role it accords to the public sphere, a role comprising both the formal processes of deliberation within constitutional institutions such as parliament and the courts and the informal discussion and debate within society at large, as it is mediated by the press and other organs of information and opinion. This model rests on the controversial empirical assumption that suitably open discussions of political issues can lead to convergence on reasonable public opinions, which are in turn capable of influencing the political process. In other words, it assumes that an appropriately structured system of public communication can have a 'rationalizing' effect on political decision-making and thus on the political organization of society in general, and it can thereby enhance the legitimacy of legislation and administration and strengthen bonds of social solidarity. In Chapter 9, 'Political Communication in Media Society', Habermas offers one of his most detailed analyses to date of the empirical data that tend to support these conclusions and of how reasonable and politically influential public opinions can arise under contemporary conditions of mass communication.

The question which the deliberative model raises for the process of European integration (and, by extension, for the model of a constitutionalization of international law) is whether the rationalizing function which Habermas ascribes to public communication can also operate above the national level. For example, one of the contentious issues in the controversy between Eurosceptics and integrationists is over whether a European-wide public sphere is possible. At first sight, the empirical realities of the European politics would seem to preclude such a possibility. Until now, European politics has been conducted within the member states largely in terms of national issues, with little mutual influence between debates in the different countries. Then, of course, there is the issue of the multilingual character of the Union: how could a joint public sphere develop among a European population divided by a multiplicity of different languages? A possible answer would be through the emergence of a higher-level European public sphere, superimposed on the existing national spheres, in which issues would be aired and discussed in a shared second language (presumably English). However, Habermas rejects this 'layered cake' model as unworkable and undesirable. It is not clear whether it is even realizable – for example, how large a readership could an English-language European daily newspaper be expected to command? But, even if the model could be realized, it would almost inevitably be confined to an educated elite, who could be expected to master English sufficiently well to engage in or with political debates, and it would endanger one of the most attractive features of the EU: its cultural diversity. The solution lies instead, Habermas argues, in the existing national public spheres becoming responsive, and thus 'permeable', to one another through the activity of cultural and journalistic translators and mediators. The key factor in communicative legitimation on the deliberative model is not that everyone across Europe should read the same newspapers and watch the same television programs, but that they should address the same issues simultaneously, in more or less the same terms. This requires only that people in one member state should be informed about, and be able to respond to – and hence, potentially, to influence – debates over issues of joint concern in the other member states.

In these brief prefatory remarks I have been able to touch on only a portion of the issues discussed in these essays. Readers from a variety of backgrounds and disciplines – or simply those who, whatever their view of Habermas's theoretical program, are curious about the recent intellectual biography of one of the most influential thinkers of our time – will find much to interest them in these essays: his deeply personal and intellectually engaging leave-taking from his friend and colleague, Richard Rorty, in the first essay; the extraordinary *rapprochement* with a thinker, Jacques Derrida, who for decades seemed to be his antipode – and a subversive critique of Heidegger – in the second; an homage to a major American public intellectual, Ronald Dworkin, in the third; the wide-ranging discussions of European politics in the second part and the extension of his models of deliberative democracy and of the public sphere to the global level in the third part; and the breathtaking survey of recent global political development, which strikes some familiar chords while eschewing triumphalism, in the closing interview. Taken together, these essays provide further impressive testimony to the undiminished vitality and creativity of critical thinking in the tradition of the Enlightenment.

A Note on the Translation

A few chapters from the corresponding German volume, *Ach, Europa* (Suhrkamp Verlag, 2008), have been omitted from the English edition, which includes instead a number of texts written since the appearance of the German counterpart (specifically, Chapters 5 and 7 and the 'Afterword' of the present volume). Readers should keep in mind that the translation contains numerous departures from the literal meaning of the German texts, which the author introduced into earlier English versions and which have been retained here with his consent. Generally these involve deletions or insertions of words or short phrases, but in some cases the author has added longer passages. Among the numerous problems posed by the translation, just one seems to merit special mention here: the key term *'Weltinnenpolitik'* has been translated either as 'global/world domestic *politics*' or as 'global/ world domestic *policy*' depending on whether the emphasis seemed to be on the *negotiation institutions and procedures* which the author proposes at the transnational level or on the *policies* which would be agreed upon in the envisaged negotiation system.

Part I
Portraits

1

'... And to define America, her athletic Democracy': In Memory of Richard Rorty*

In view of the highly personal occasion that brings us together today, please allow me to begin with a private recollection.

I first encountered Richard Rorty at a conference on Heidegger held in San Diego in 1974. At the opening of the conference, a video of an interview with the absent Herbert Marcuse was screened in which he described his relationship with Heidegger in the early 1930s in milder terms than the sharp post-war correspondence between them would have led one to expect. Much to my annoyance, this set the tone of unpolitical veneration of Heidegger that prevailed throughout the entire conference. Only Marjorie Green, who had also studied in Freiburg prior to 1933, made a brusque comment to the effect that, at the time, at most the closer circle of Heidegger students, to which Marcuse belonged, could have been deceived as to the true political outlook of their mentor.

In this ambivalent mood I then heard a professor from Princeton, who was until then known to me only as the editor of a celebrated collection of essays on the linguistic turn,[1] put forward a provocative comparison. He tried to harmonize the dissonant voices of three world-famous

---

*Address to a memorial service held at Stanford University on 2 November 2007.

3

soloists in a strange concert: Dewey, the radical democrat and the most political among the pragmatists, featured in this chorus alongside Heidegger, the very embodiment of the arrogant German mandarin par excellence. The third member of this unequal alliance was Wittgenstein, from whose *Philosophical Investigations* I had learnt so much; but he, too, was not completely free of the prejudices of the German ideology with its intellectual fetishism, and he cut a strange figure alongside Dewey.[2]

Certainly, from the perspective of Humboldt and philosophical hermeneutics, a consideration of the world-disclosing function of language reveals an original affinity between Heidegger and Wittgenstein. This discovery must have fascinated Rorty, once he had been convinced by Thomas Kuhn to read the history of science in contextualist terms. But how did Dewey, the embodiment of the democratic wing of the Young Hegelians that we so sorely lacked in Europe, fit into this constellation? Dewey's way of thinking, if anyone's, stood in stark contrast to the German–Hellenistic pretentiousness, to the lofty tone and elitist arrogance of the few who claim a privileged access to truth against the many.

At that time, I found the juxtaposition so obscene that I lost my composure in the discussion. Surprisingly enough, the distinguished colleague from Princeton was not in the least irritated by the robust protest from the German backwoods; he was instead so kind as to invite me to his seminar. For me, that visit to Princeton marked the beginning of a friendship as happy and rewarding as it was instructive. On the bedrock of shared political convictions we could express and accept our philosophical differences with ease. Thus something of the 'priority of politics over philosophy' for which Dick also explicitly argued with me proved itself in practice and served as a tacit basis of our ongoing relationship. As regards Heidegger, incidentally, my initial agitation proved to be unfounded. Dick likewise felt a greater affinity with the pragmatist Heidegger of the early sections of *Being and*

Time than with the esoteric thinker who hearkened to the voice of Being.[3]

Following our first meeting, Dick sent me an offprint of his essay 'The World well Lost',[4] whose title's ironic allusion should have already alerted me to the intellectual and writer behind the philosopher Richard Rorty. However, I read the essay, with its rigorous analytical argumentation, in the way one tends to read articles from the *Journal of Philosophy*. Only with hindsight did I realize that it was a preliminary draft of the critique of the modern paradigm of epistemology he was to publish a couple of years later as *Philosophy and the Mirror of Nature* (1979), a book destined to have such an unprecedented impact. What was revolutionary in this study was less the critical reconstruction of the linguistic turn, taken in different ways by Heidegger and by Wittgenstein, than the insistence on one crucial consequence of the shift from 'consciousness' to 'language'. Rorty systematically deconstructed the spectator model of 'representative' or 'fact-depicting' thinking. This critique struck at the heart of a discipline which, since Russell and Carnap, was preoccupied with achieving scientific respectability through a logical and semantic treatment of fundamental epistemological issues, first raised during the seventeenth century. Allow me to remind you briefly of the key issue here. If facts cannot be conceived independently of the propositional structure of our language and if the truth of opinions and statements can be corrected only by other opinions and statements, then any idea of truth as correspondence between sentences and facts 'out there' is misleading. We cannot describe nature in a language we assume to be nature's own language. On the pragmatist interpretation, the 'depiction' of reality is replaced by a problem-solving 'coping' with the challenges of an over-complex world. In other words, we acquire our knowledge of facts through our constructive dealings with a disconcerting environment. Nature provides only indirect answers, because all of its answers remain bound to the grammar of our questions. What we call 'the world', therefore, does not consist of the totality of facts. Instead it is the sum total of the cognitively relevant constraints to which our attempts to learn from, and to achieve control over, contingent natural processes through reliable predictions are subject.

Rorty's painstaking analysis of the assumed representative function of the knowing mind can command respect even from those colleagues who are not willing to follow the ambitious thrust of the author's conclusions. This ambition was revealed at the time by an addition to the English title in the German translation: *Philosophy and the Mirror of Nature* appeared in German under the title: *The Mirror of Nature*, with the subtitle: *A Critique of Philosophy* (tout court!). I myself first grasped the full scope of Rorty's project, and thus the meaning behind that strange constellation of Heidegger, Wittgenstein, and Dewey, when I read the introduction to his essay collection *Consequences of Pragmatism* (1982).

For those who knew the author in person it was not easy to bring the extraordinary claims of this philosopher, writer, and political intellectual into line with the modest, shy, and sensitive character of the person of the same name. His public appearances were marked by rhetorical brilliance, controlled passion, the charm of a youthful, at times sharply polemical mind, indeed by a certain pathos. For deflation and understatement can acquire a pathos of their own. But behind the aura of the impressive speaker and writer and of the passionate teacher lay concealed that quiet, reserved, noble, and loveable man who hated nothing more than any pretence of profundity. Yet, for all our reverence for the personality of our friend, we should not downplay the ambition of the philosophical claims he championed.

Richard Rorty's aim was nothing less than to foster a culture which liberated itself from the conceptual obsessions of Greek philosophy – and from a fetishism of science which sprang from the furrows of that metaphysics. What he understood by 'metaphysics' and what he criticized about it can best be seen if we bear in mind what underlies this critique: 'Philosophers became preoccupied with images of the future only after they gave up the hope of gaining knowledge of the eternal.'[5] Platonism fixes its gaze on the immutable Forms of the good and of the true and spawns a web of categorical distinctions in which the creative energies of a self-generating human species ossify. Of course, Rorty did not regard the priority of essence over appearance, of the universal over the particular, of necessity over contingency, and of nature over history as purely theoretical matters. Because these concern how ways of life are structured, he sought to familiarize his contemporaries with a vocabulary which articulates a different view of the world and of ourselves.

Rorty's hope was that a second, more radical phase of the Enlightenment would rejuvenate the authentic motives of a modernity which had lost its way. For modernity must discover the source of all normativity within itself. There is no longer any authority or foundation beyond the opaque ebb and flow of contingencies. Nobody can leave her local context without finding herself in a different one. At the same time, the human condition is such that the sober recognition of the finitude and corruptibility of human beings – of the fallibility of the mind, the vulnerability of the body, and the fragility of social bonds – can and should become the driving force behind the creativity of a restless self-transformation of society and culture. Against this backdrop, Rorty believes that we must learn to see ourselves as the children of a self-confident modernity, if Walt Whitman's faith in a better future is to have any chance in our politically, economically, and socially divided world society. The democratic voice of hope in a fraternal and inclusive form of social life must not fall silent.

The moving songs of the public intellectual Richard Rorty – his interviews and lectures, his popular message of 'contingency, irony, and solidarity', the treatises that were disseminated worldwide – are all infused with the

7

peculiarly romantic and highly personal harmonic triad of meta-philosophy, neo-pragmatism, and leftist patriotism. For this life and work I can think of no more fitting epitaph than a quotation from a poem by Walt Whitman dating from 1871. Under the title *To Foreign Lands*, these are words that Dick might also have addressed to his European friends:

> I heard that you ask'd for something to prove this puzzle the New World,
> And to define America, her athletic Democracy,
> Therefore I send you my poems that you behold in them what you wanted.[6]

You have invited a philosophical colleague to speak for this hour. Thus you can expect me to try to explain how Richard Rorty proceeded from that 'metacritique of knowledge'[7] to which I referred above to a critique of metaphysics, and from there to the cosmopolitan patriotism of a very American democrat.

The pragmatist conception of knowledge that Rorty develops in *The Mirror of Nature* should be seen in the context of a Hegelian naturalism. From this perspective, the initial conditions for a culture created by human beings are the result of natural evolution. All past cultural achievements can be construed in functional terms as 'tools' which have proved their worth in practical and instrumental interactions with risk-laden environments. This way of looking at anthropology and history inspires at most a 'soft' naturalism. The Darwinist language does not undermine the everyday self-understanding of socialized individuals as autonomous, creative actors who are capable of learning and are socialized through norms. By contrast, this very line between soft and hard naturalism is crossed by those reductionist explanations which combine insights from biogenetics and neurology in a speculative manner, in the context of neo-Darwinist evolutionary theory. They overstep the boundary of a naturalist self-objectification of man beyond which we can no longer understand ourselves as the authors of our actions, discoveries, and inventions. The 'self' disappears under the sway of such objectivistic self-descriptions if they purport to be the only true ones. They treat as an illusion the very thing which Rorty's interpretation of neo-pragmatism as a kind of *Lebensphilosophie* so celebrates in human beings, namely the consciousness of freedom, creativity, and learning.

This turn towards scientism could not fail to inspire Rorty's protest. Because he spelled out his own concept of human beings in Darwinist terms, he had to introduce a stop rule into this kind of soft naturalism. In order to be in a position to reject the hard naturalism of a Daniel Dennett as 'scientism', he needed an explanation for the ideological inflation of objectivizing research approaches into a pseudo-scientific objectivism. He hoped to find such an explanation by embedding the spectator model of knowledge in a sweeping deconstruction of the history of metaphysics. Within this broader context he discovered a certain affinity between scientism and Platonism. Both share the bad habit of conceiving of human knowledge as a kind of passive reflection, thus relocating the subjects of this knowledge beyond the limits of our, or indeed any, world: 'The last line of defense for essentialist philosophers is the belief that physical science gets us outside ourselves, outside our language and our purposes to something splendidly nonhuman and nonrelational.'[8] With the aid of Heidegger's and Wittgenstein's critique of the onto-logical implications of the language of physicalism, Rorty claims to find traces of the Platonic heritage of the search for a view from nowhere, for an objective standpoint of self-observation outside the world, in the reductionist explanatory strategies of cognitive scientists and biologists.

Of course, the price Rorty pays for his critique of meta-physics is an anti-realism, a price which Dewey did not pay in his key anti-Platonist text, *Reconstruction in*

Philosophy (1920). Rorty felt that he had to complement soft naturalism with a radical historicism if he wanted to avoid slipping into scientism. He felt that a modern culture capable of standing on its own feet could avoid the pull of scientistic self-reification only by rejecting two things: the assumption that an objective world exists independently of our descriptions; and the inner-worldly transcendence of universal, context-independent claims to validity. The standards of rationality to which we performatively lay claim are also subject to the ups and downs of cultural practices.

Rorty may have found it easy to take this plausible, though rather controversial, step because he found Heidegger's deconstruction appealing for another reason. There is a streak of nostalgia about a philosophy which claims to make a clean break with all extant philosophy, a nostalgia born of disappointment with the unredeemed promises of metaphysics. This melancholic gesture of leave-taking and surpassing betrays a Platonist motivation underlying Rorty's and Heidegger's anti-Platonism. Rorty bemoans the state of a discipline which retains the name of philosophy but has forfeited any of its public relevance. In particular, the analytical orthodoxy in which Rorty himself was trained has accelerated philosophy's transformation into a highly specialized and compartmentalized discipline. Here only the questions posed by the profession are regarded as serious, no longer those posed by 'life'. Rorty was troubled by this development as early as 1967, and it pained him. Already then, his doubts concerning the state of the discipline led him to taunt the profession by denying even its basic presupposition 'that there are philosophical truths to be discovered and demonstrated by argument'.[9] A quite different perspective opens up if we ask what can or should remain of philosophy after the end of metaphysics.

In Rorty's view, the critique of Platonism can give rise only to a philosophy which has an historical understanding of itself and captures its own age in thought, in other words one which continues the discourse of modernity initiated by Hegel. At this point, however, Rorty's and Heidegger's paths diverge. Rorty was never tempted to pursue the arrogant, exalted self-celebration of a form of recollective thinking [*Andenken*] which could dispense with all argumentation. Like Dewey, he engaged in two discourses simultaneously, one with his fellow philosophers, on technical questions, and the other with the general public, on issues relating to the self-understanding of modernity. He conducted the latter, exoteric, discourse in Wittgenstein's therapeutic vein. Once the human mind becomes ensnared in the conceptual network of Platonism, no theory can help to cure this pathogenic self-misunderstanding, only the deflation of misguided theoretical claims can. This accounts for a typical trait in Rorty's public appearances: his rhetoric of debunking, of 'forget it', of shrugging off or filing away, his suggestion that an issue be 'dropped' because it 'has become uninteresting'.

The anti-Platonist thrust is directed against an inflated self-image which, because of an imagined participation in the ideal, super-human world, in fact makes us into slaves of these idols. Rorty fought against our Platonist compulsion to deceive ourselves about the merely conventional and contingent aspects of daily life; in this respect he always shared the trivializing and egalitarian convictions of the pragmatists. But Wittgenstein's style of therapy also had to take a back seat to Dewey's democratic commitment, because Rorty's therapeutic practice was meant to have a transforming and liberating character, not the quietistic and thus conservative sense of restoring an untroubled *status quo ante*. The dual hostile stance against metaphysics and against scientism follows objectives for which Rorty coined effective slogans. He defends the 'priority of democracy over philosophy' and the 'priority of technology over theory'. Philosophy and the sciences must make themselves useful, now that their success can no longer be measured in terms of whether statements correspond to a reality unsullied by language and culture. What counts is the contribution which philosophical and scientific practice can make to a continually expanding consensus on basic human interests and on the means to satisfy the individual diversity of competing human needs. Just as theory-building in the natural sciences subserves its possible technical success, so philosophy subserves democracy and freedom: 'if we take care of political freedom, we get truth as a bonus'.[10] Be that as it may, philosophy can play a public role through reflection on the pressing problems of the day – reflection informed by a sensitive diagnosis of the times. In America Richard Rorty was virtually unrivalled in restoring philosophy's public importance. Whether his colleagues thank him for that is another matter.

However, a philosopher who takes on the role of a public intellectual can have recourse neither to the expert knowledge of the natural and social sciences nor even to the historical and aesthetic knowledge accumulated in the humanities. In his public interventions, Rorty made a virtue of these shortcomings by turning the task of philosophy itself into a topic. He developed meta-philosophical reflections and confronted 'scientific' philosophers with those who take their cue from literature. Like Nietzsche, he pondered on the benefits and drawbacks of classical education, though in his own way:

> All of these wonderful books are only rungs on a ladder that, with a bit of luck, one day we may be able to do without. If we stopped reading canonical philosophy books, we would be less aware of the forces that make us think and talk as we do. We would be less able to grasp our contingency, less capable of being 'ironists'.[11]

So this is one task of philosophy: to instill in its addressees an awareness of the contingencies of human existence, in particular the contingencies which impact on the presumed foundations, on what we take to be our 'final' vocabularies. In this way Rorty practiced something of what the ancients called 'wisdom'. And it is no accident that he used a word for this practice which is religious in origin, namely 'edification'. Private edification is of course just one half of the business of philosophical communication. Public commitment is the other, even more important, task of philosophy. As a pragmatist, Rorty could encourage citizens and elites in the world's leading power to recall their own tradition. In the public political arena, he recommended this cultural resource as the key to interpreting the current situation.

This pragmatism is inspired by the spirit of great writers and great philosophers alike. Rorty repeatedly cites Emerson, Whitman, James, and Dewey. And because this spirit is aware of its American origins and at the same time sees itself as a progressive force, all the pragmatist writers and philosophers shared the sharp profile of a leftist patriotism, that is, an enlarged cosmopolitan patriotism. Rorty had the fortunate combination of his three rare talents to thank for the fact that he could draw fully on this heritage; for he was in equal part an important philosopher, a marvelous writer, and a politically influential intellectual.

***

Let me conclude with a word on each of the roles he so gloriously mastered: of the philosopher, of the writer, and of the leftist cosmopolitan patriot. First the philosopher.

In his profession, Richard Rorty exchanged the most sophisticated arguments with his most prominent colleagues. He debated the concept of truth with Donald Davidson, he argued about realism and rationality with Hilary Putnam, about the concept of the mental with Daniel Dennet, on intersubjectivity and objectivity with John McDowell, and on the status of facts with his master student Robert Brandom.[12] On the European continent his work is as much in evidence as it is in the English-speaking world; if anything, it is perhaps even more influential in Europe. Rorty mastered the philosophical idioms of both worlds. Two of his three philosophical heroes were Europeans, after all. With his interpretive skills he did great service for Foucault and Derrida not only in the United States, but also in Germany. And it was he who served as the mediator of our indirect communication when we, in Europe, had problems in reaching an understanding between the parties on either side of the Rhine.

As to the writer, we have to acknowledge that, among those rare philosophers who can write flawless scholarly prose, Richard Rorty came closest to the spirit of poetry. His strategy of an eye-opening renovation of philosophical jargon underlies the affinity between his texts and the world-disclosing power of literature. Over the decades, no other colleague so consistently surprised me with new ideas and exciting formulations as he did. Rorty overwhelms his readers with mind-boggling rearrangements of conceptual constellations and shocks them with unexpected oppositions. The barbaric simplifications into which he seems to cobble together complex trains of thought prove at second glance to contain innovative interpretations. Rorty plays with his readers' conventional expectations. Unusual series of names challenge them into rethinking connections. The thought flashes up indirectly. Sometimes it is merely a matter of emphasis. If he names Donald Davidson, Daniel Dennett, Annette Baier, and Robert Brandom in a single breath, then the imperceptible discrepancy which disconcerts the reader is the real message – in this case, the reference to Annette Baier's masterly reconstruction of Hume's moral philosophy, which Rorty wishes to highlight as an 'intellectual advance'.

Finally, in Rorty we encounter an old-fashioned sort of leftist intellectual, who believes in education and social reform. What he regards as most important in a democratic constitution is that it provides the encumbered and oppressed with instruments through which they 'can defend themselves against the wealthy and the powerful'.

14

The primary focus is on abolishing institutions which perpetuate exploitation and degradation. The aim is to promote a tolerant society, which unites people in solidarity in spite of increasing diversity and recognizes as binding no authority which cannot be derived from deliberation and revisable agreements among all concerned. Rorty described himself, in Todd Gitlin's words, as a 'red diaper anticommunist baby' who became a teenage Cold War liberal.[13] But that past did not leave the slightest trace of resentment in him. He was completely free of the scars so typical of former radicals as well as of many of the older liberal hawks – and of some of the younger ones. If he was susceptible to any bitter political sentiment, then it was the one he directed against a cultural Left which, he felt, had abandoned the struggle: 'In so far as a Left becomes spectatorial and retrospective, it ceases to be a Left.'[14]

With *Achieving our Country*, his most personal and moving book, Richard Rorty pinned his colors to the mast of an American patriotism that the world need not fear. In the melody of this text we find a combination of the exceptional status of the world's oldest democracy – one which can be proud of the normative substance of its principles – and of the receptiveness to the new and now global diversity of cultural perspectives and voices. What is new about this global pluralism compared to the strained pluralism of a national society is the fact that, within the inclusive frame of an encompassing international community, the dangers of disintegration can no longer be cleverly deflected onto an external enemy. Today, evolutionary anthropology, with its comparative research on children and chimpanzees of the same age, is recuperating an old pragmatist insight when it rediscovers 'perspective-taking' as an ability which is exclusive to human beings. Bertolt Brecht makes reciprocal perspective-taking into the essential condition of genuine patriotism:

And because we are tending to this land,
May we love and protect it.

15

And may it seem to us the dearest,
Just as to others their own land seems.

Dick knew those lines from the famous 'Children's Hymn', and he knew that, even for a superpower, cosmopolitanism is not the same thing as the global export of its own way of life. He knew that a democracy can preserve its robust and 'athletic' character only through self-criticism. In an interview conducted on 11 September 2001 he warned against Bush's 'arrogant anti-internationalism'. He reminded us instead of the idea which had prompted an American president in the wake of the horrors of the Second World War to envisage a new design for a future world order and to push for the establishment of the United Nations. Yet Rorty was not unrealistic in his view of things: 'That scenario now sounds less plausible. But it is the only one I can envisage that might actually have good results.' And he then added a sentence which expresses the spirit of this person, and also the spirit of the best tradition his country has brought forth: 'There is, to be sure, plenty of reason for pessimism, but it would be better to do what one can to get people to follow an improbable scenario than to simply throw up one's hands.'[15]

That spirit is to be found throughout Richard Rorty's works, and will continue to live through them.

2
How to Answer the Ethical Question: Derrida and Religion*

(1)   I would like to express my gratitude for this opportunity to participate in a conference on the Jewish background of Jacques Derrida's philosophy. My distance from the essential topics to be dealt with here already means that I will have to limit myself to a marginal contribution. For, in spite of my long association with Gershom Scholem, I am no expert in the field of Judaism,[1] and in the present group I am certainly the one with the least familiarity with Derrida's work as a whole. Of course, Derrida would be the first to object that marginality is not necessarily a disadvantage.

Be that as it may; I had two reasons for accepting the invitation. I would like to express my respect for a body of work in which I recognize from a certain distance motives and intentions I share. In addition, I would like to take the opportunity to pose a question to Jacques Derrida which has preoccupied me for a long time: At what point exactly does Derrida's thought part ways with that of Heidegger? I don't mean this in just a philological sense; the question is as much a philosophical as a political one.

* Lecture delivered at the conference 'Judéités, questions pour Jacques Derrida', held on 3–5 November 2000 in the Jewish Community Centre in Paris in Derrida's presence.

Last summer in Frankfurt, Derrida delivered a lecture on the topic which we in Germany call 'the idea of the university'.[2] It was a passionate plea for the unconditional obligation of the academic community to seek the truth and to defend freedom. Derrida argued that, if a university is to remain true to its very idea, it must provide the intellectual space for such a profession of faith [*Bekenntnis*]. It is the task of 'professors' to reaffirm constantly the performative meaning of this 'profession of faith', namely the 'putting into effect' ['*Ins-Werk-Setzen*'] of the truth. The formula used by Derrida is reminiscent of the world-disclosing function which Heidegger ascribes chiefly to the great works of literature, art, and philosophy. Thus it was no surprise that Derrida devoted the final part of his lecture – albeit in the necessarily ironic tone of an invocation – to an act of evocation: to the 'advent of the event' [*'Ankunft des Ereignisses'*].

Derrida was speaking in a lecture hall, and thus *intra muros*. As a consequence, the invocation was a self-referential gesture intended to encourage the audience to defend 'the walls' of university:

> It is too often said that the performative produces the event of which it speaks. One must also realize that, inversely, where there is a performance, an event worthy of the name cannot arise. If what arrives belongs to the horizon of the possible, or even of a possible performative … it does not arrive, it does not happen, in the full sense of the word. As I have tried to demonstrate, only the impossible can arrive … The force of the event is always stronger than the force of a performative.[3]

Derrida's words sound like an echo of those dark words which we know from Heidegger's work *Of Enowning* [*Vom Ereignis*]. Between 1936 and 1938 Heidegger devoted himself for the first time to overcoming the totalitarian features of a power-obsessed subjectivism through thinking. Heidegger first made this 'turn' public in 1946. In the *Letter on Humanism* he declares his unequivocal rejection of the letter and spirit of the 'humanist' tradition which has shaped the self-interpretation of modernity. My impression, though, is that Derrida wishes to rescue the essence of this 'humanism', although he espouses Heidegger's posture towards the 'advent of the event'.

Derrida invokes the global implementation of human rights and the prosecution of crimes against humanity, and he advocates a form of democracy which transcends national frontiers and a sovereignty freed from false connotations. The appeal to autonomy, the incitement to resistance and to civil disobedience – everything that Derrida associates with his profession of faith in the idea of the university – all of these constitute arguments against Heidegger's condemnation of humanism. Simply put, my question is: How does Derrida's understanding of the advent of a portentous 'event', which nevertheless remains indeterminate, differ from Heidegger's? Is there some difference which explains their positions for and against 'humanism'? We must not trivialize the substantial question I have in mind into a mere terminological one. Nothing much hangs on whether we use the term 'humanism' in a positive or in a negative sense. The issue concerns humanism itself: what Derrida invokes as a *telos*, Heidegger treats with contempt. My suspicion is that their views diverge over the unswerving loyalty to a specific content of the monotheistic heritage – and over the neo-pagan betrayal of this heritage.[4] Let me recall what Gershom Scholem has to say about this loyalty: 'Genuine traditions remain hidden; only a declining tradition deteriorates into an object and its greatness first becomes apparent in the process of decline.'[5]

Since I am aware that my knowledge of Derrida's ramified work is limited, I propose to take a detour and start from a distant place. You must not expect an exegesis or an exercise in deconstruction, or even a close reading. In what follows, I will first explain the modern distinction between morality and ethics (2); I will then present Kierkegaard's postmetaphysical but Christian answer to

the 'basic ethical question' (3) and discuss various philosophical attempts to assimilate in a postreligious spirit
Kierkegaard's ethical insights (4); and finally I will present
some arguments which will enable me to formulate my
question to Derrida more precisely (5).

(2) 'Ethics' at one time meant the doctrine of the 'correct
life'. In the shadow cast by the Second World War, Adorno
had good reasons for presenting his *Minima Moralia* as
'melancholic science', as *Reflections on a Damaged Life*. As
long as philosophy still believed itself capable of compre-
hending nature and history as a whole, it could fall back
on a supposedly stable framework to which life, both
individual and communal, had to conform. The structure
of the cosmos and of human nature, the stages of world
history and of the history of salvation supplied normatively imbued 'facts' which seemed to offer insight into
the correct conduct of life. 'Correct' here had the exemplary meaning of a model of individual and communal
political life worthy of emulation. The doctrines of the
good life and of the just society – ethics and politics – were
still all of a piece. But, with the accelerating pace of social
change, the expiration date of these models of the ethical
life has become shorter, no matter whether they took their
cue from the Greek polis, from the orders of the mediae-
val *societas civilis*, from the universal individual of the
Renaissance cities, or, as in Hegel, from the structure of
the family, civil society, and constitutional monarchy.

John Rawls's political liberalism marks the end of this
development.[6] Rawls responded to the pluralism of worldviews and to the progressive individualization of lifestyles.
He drew the consequence from the failure of philosophical attempts to privilege certain ways of life as exemplary
or as universally binding. The just society guarantees each
individual equal freedom to develop an ethical self-
understanding as a precondition for realizing a personal
conception of the good life in accordance with her abilities
and preferences.

Of course, practical philosophy does not dispense with normative considerations altogether. But it limits itself for the most part to questions of justice. We regard norms and actions from the 'moral point of view' when it is a question of determining what is equally in the interest of each individual and what is equally good for all. Moral theory and ethics seem at first sight to be concerned with the same question: 'What should I or what should we do?' But the 'should' takes on a different meaning when it is no longer a question, as judged from an inclusive 'we'-perspective, of the rights and duties which individuals ascribe to one another but of what is best 'for me' or 'for us' in the long run, all things considered, judged from a first-person perspective informed by concern for one's own life. For such ethical questions concerning one's own well-being arise in the context of a particular life history or a particular form of life. They are closely bound up with questions of identity: How should we understand ourselves, who we are and who we want to be, while still being able to look at ourselves in the mirror?

The analytic differentiation between the two spheres leads to a separation between theories of justice and morality on the one side, and theories of 'ethics', understood in the classical sense of a doctrine of the correct or good life, on the other. The moral point of view requires us to abstract from the exemplary images a successful, or not-misspent, life handed down in the great metaphysical and religious narratives. It may be that the substance of these 'strong traditions' still nourishes our existential self-understanding; but philosophy can no longer intervene in the conflict between these belief systems on its own account. Precisely in the questions which remain of greatest relevance for us, therefore, it shifts to a meta-level and confines itself to examining the formal features of communicative processes without taking a position of its own on their contents.

Moral, legal, and political theories pay a high price for their division of labor with an 'ethics' which henceforth focuses exclusively on the *form* of processes of existential self-understanding. They dissolve the connection that first lends moral judgments their capacity to motivate actors to act in the right way. Moral insights bind the will effectively only when they are embedded in an ethical self-understanding which harnesses the concern for one's own welfare on behalf of the interest in justice. However well deontological theories may explain how moral norms should be justified and applied, they cannot answer the question as to why we should act morally in the first place. Political theories are no better at explaining why democratic citizens should take their orientation from the common good in conflicts over principles of social interaction instead of making do with a utilitarian modus vivendi. The most that theories of justice uncoupled from ethics can hope for is that processes of socialization and political forms of life will 'meet them halfway'.

Even more disturbing is the question of why philosophical ethics should abandon the field to psychotherapy, for example, which has no compunction to take on the classic task of providing existential orientation in remedying psychic disturbances. The concept of 'psychic illness' rests on an analogy with physical illness. But how far does the analogy go, given that there are scarcely any psychological analogues to the clearly discernible indicators of the healthy state of the body? Evidently a normative conception of an 'undisturbed relation to self' must take the place of the missing somatic indicators. This is especially apparent in cases where the psychological suffering which forces the patient to consult an analyst is itself repressed, so that the disturbance fits inconspicuously into normal life. Why should philosophy balk at something which psychoanalysis takes for granted? The issue here is to clarify our intuitive understanding of the clinical features of a misspent or non-misspent life.

(3) Kierkegaard was the first thinker to answer the basic ethical question concerning the success or failure of one's

life in terms of a postmetaphysical conception of 'being able to be oneself'. This level of abstraction reflects the challenge of the dominant pluralism concerning world-views in our societies. In *Either/Or*, Kierkegaard contrasts the 'ethical' with the 'aesthetic' conception of life. Not without sympathy, he depicts in the bright colors of the early romantic era the image of a casually ironic, drifting, egocentric, and playful existence devoted to the refined enjoyment of the moment. The desired contrast to this hedonism is a resolute ethical conduct of life which requires the individual to collect himself and to free himself from the dependencies of an overpowering surrounding world. The individual must rouse himself to an awareness of his individuality and freedom. He must retrieve himself from the anonymous distraction of a breathless, fragmented existence and lend continuity and transparency to his life. A person who has become self-aware in this way 'has himself as a task which is set for him even though it has become his through his having chosen it'.[7]

Kierkegaard tacitly assumes that the individual who lives in a self-conscious way continually accounts for his life in the light of the Sermon on the Mount. He wastes few words on the moral standards which found a secular expression in Kant's egalitarian universalism. His complete attention is devoted instead to the structure of being-able-to-be-oneself – that is, to the form of an ethical reflection on, and choice of, self which is determined by the 'infinite interest in the success' of one's own life plan. The individual self-critically appropriates the past of his factually given and concretely recollected life history, with a view to future possibilities of action. Only in this way does he transform himself into an irreplaceable person and a unique individual.

Through a scrupulous moral evaluation and critical appropriation of his factual life history, he constitutes himself as the person he simultaneously is and would like to be: 'Everything posited with his freedom belongs to

him essentially, however accidental it may seem ...' Of
course, Kierkegaard is far removed from Sartre's existen-
tialism when he adds:

> However, for the ethical individual, this distinction is not
> the product of whim ... For although [he] may refer to
> himself as his own editor, he is at the same time fully
> aware of his editorial responsibility to himself ... to the
> scheme of things in which he lives, and to God.[8]

Kierkegaard is convinced that the ethical mode of existence which each individual generates from out of himself
can be stabilized only in the believer's relation to God. He
goes beyond speculative philosophy and thus thinks in a
postmetaphysical, though not at all in a postreligious, way.
The ethical question can find a binding answer only if
moral knowledge is supplemented by faith. If morality
could move the will of the knowing subject through good
reasons alone, the desolate condition which Kierkegaard
consistently denounces in his capacity of social critic would
be inexplicable – namely the condition of an enlightened
Christian and self-righteously moral society which is nevertheless deeply corrupt. The normalized repression and
cynical recognition of an unjust world do not point to a
lack of knowledge, but to a corruption of the will. Those
who should know better refuse to understand. This is why
Kierkegaard does not speak of guilt but of sin.

Once we interpret guilt as sin, however, we know that
we depend on forgiveness and must pin our hopes on an
absolute power, which can intervene retroactively in the
course of history and re-establish the violated order and
integrity of the victims. (This was the subject of a famous
debate between Benjamin and Horkheimer in the 1930s.)
Only the promise of salvation can provide the motivational link between unconditional moral obligation and
the concern for one's own well-being. Kierkegaard plays
out the problem of motivation against Socrates and Kant
in order to go beyond both of them and reach Christ.

However, Climacus – the pseudonymous author of the *Philosophical Fragments* – is not at all sure that the Christian message of salvation, which he treats hypothetically as a 'thought project', is 'truer' than the immanent mode of thought which moves within the postmetaphysical bounds of worldview neutrality.[9] This is why Kierkegaard introduces an Anti-Climacus. Although the latter cannot defeat his secular adversary with arguments, he would like to prompt him to 'go beyond a Socrates' with the help of a psychological phenomenology.[10]

Kierkegaard employs a symptomatology of forms of life to describe the stages of a salutary 'sickness onto death'. These comprise the different forms assumed by a despair which is initially repressed, but then enters consciousness and in the end compels an inversion of egocentric consciousness. These forms of despair are manifestations of the failure of a basic existential relationship which only an authentic relation to oneself could make possible. Kierkegaard depicts the disturbing condition of a person who, although he is aware that it is his unavoidable destiny to be a self, nevertheless takes refuge in the alternatives: 'in despair not to will to be oneself. Or even lower: in despair not to will to be a self. Or lowest of all: in despair to will to be someone else ...'[11] One who in the end recognizes that the source of despair does not lie in external conditions but in his attempts at flight will make the defiant – but equally unsuccessful – attempt 'to will to be oneself'. The despairing failure of this final effort of will – of this completely single-minded wanting-to-be-oneself – moves the finite spirit to transcend itself and to recognize its dependency on an Other in which its freedom is grounded.

This reversal is supposed to mark the turning point of the exercise, the overcoming of the secularized self-understanding of modern reason. Kierkegaard uses a formula to describe this rebirth which is reminiscent of the first paragraphs of Fichte's *Doctrine of Science*, even though at the same time it inverts the autonomous meaning of the act into its opposite: 'in relating to itself and in willing to be itself, the self rests transparently in the power that established it'.[12] This reveals the fundamental relationship which makes 'being-a-self' the correct mode of life from the perspective of the religious author. Although the literal reference to a 'power' on which being-able-to-be-oneself is founded need not be understood in a religious sense, Kierkegaard insists on the fact that the human spirit can arrive at the correct understanding of its finite existence only through the awareness of sinfulness. The self truly exists only in the face of God. It survives the stages of hopeless despair only in the shape of a believer who, in relating to himself, relates to an absolute Other to whom he owes everything.[13]

(4) Kierkegaard was obsessed throughout his life by the Lutheran question of divine mercy. This orthodoxy is, of course, a source of irritation for his philosophical successors. Kierkegaard insists that we cannot form a consistent concept of God either *via eminentiae* or *via negationis*. Every idealization remains captive to the finite basic predicates from which the operation of amplification begins; and the attempt of the understanding to define the absolute Other by negating all finite determinations also fails for the same reason. '[T]he understanding cannot even think the absolutely different; it cannot absolutely negate itself, but uses itself for that purpose and consequently thinks the difference in itself.'[14] It is not possible to bridge the chasm between knowledge and faith through thought. This is a major obstacle for secular philosophers who would like to follow Kierkegaard in the postmetaphysical approach to ethics even though they cannot accept revelation in any sense. In this connection I would first like to consider Jaspers and Sartre briefly, before turning to Heidegger and Adorno.

Karl Jaspers conceives of philosophical knowledge as a form of faith, namely as faith in reason. Philosophy rejects revelation as a source of truth, yet it stands in competition with religious teachings when it comes to the correct normative self-understanding of individuals and communities, indeed of humanity as a whole. Socrates is elevated, as it were, to the same level as Christ.[15] This strategic conceptual move entails the difficult task of explaining the paradoxical intermediary position of philosophy between faith and science, and hence the status of an epistemic undertaking described in these terms. How is a philosophy which must obey the normal standards of rational discourse nevertheless supposed to share the domain of transcendent questions and dogmatic claims with the major world religions?[16]

The modal resemblance between postmetaphysical thinking and faith is no more plausible than the juxtaposition between philosophy and science. Since the high Middle Ages, philosophy, for all its diversity, has consistently upheld its scientific character – philosophy and science inhabit a single universe of rational discourse. By contrast, Jean-Paul Sartre adopts a different, avowedly atheistic strategy in drawing upon the legacy of Kierkegaard's existential dialectics.

However, Sartre's conception of freedom blurs the boundary between a self-confident ethical mode of life and a defiant self-assertive subjectivism. The critique of the groundlessness of this self-assertion is the key to Kierkegaard's phenomenology of the self-generating stages of despair. Like Kierkegaard, Sartre wants to take account of the fallibilism of the human mind and of the unconditional character of moral claims. But he distances himself from Kierkegaard's plausible argument that the self, on the hypothesis of a self-projecting freedom, cannot hope to do justice to the ethical claim to unconditionality because the self-reliant subject repudiates the contingency and finitude of his existence. He cannot comprehend his dependence on a power, at once enabling and justifying, which is beyond his control. The conscious ethical conduct of life must not be understood as blinkered self-empowerment.

27

A philosophy which wants to develop Kierkegaard's ethics further, through an immanent critique, must offer an interpretation of this 'enabling power'. A strict naturalistic explanation in the scientistic sense is ruled out, because the 'transparent' dependence on an Other points to an interpersonal relation. For the defiance of a rebellious individual who in the end desperately wants to be himself is directed, as defiance, against a second person. On the other hand, we cannot equate the power which escapes our control – and on which we, as subjects capable of speech and action, depend in our anxiety not to squander our lives – with Kierkegaard's 'God in time', under the premises of postmetaphysical thinking.

The linguistic turn now makes possible a deflationary interpretation of our finitude and of our dependence on an 'Other'. As historical and social beings, we are always already situated within a linguistically structured lifeworld. We encounter a transcending power in the forms of communication through which we relate to one another about something in the world and about ourselves. For language is not a private possession. Nobody can exercise exclusive control over the shared medium of communication. No participant *alone* can exert control over the structure, or even over the course, of processes of communication and of self-understanding. This reading recovers, in a weak, procedural sense, a meaning of 'unconditionality' which is at once fallible and anti-sceptical. How speakers and hearers use their communicative freedom to take 'yes' or 'no' stances is not an arbitrary or subjective matter. For they are free only in virtue of the binding power of the claims in need of justification which they raise towards one another. Thus an intersubjective power which is prior to, and underlies, the subjectivity of the speakers is embodied in the logos of language.

The logos of language escapes our control, and yet it is we, the subjects capable of speaking and acting, who communicate with one another in this medium. It remains 'our' language. Raising unconditional validity claims is a necessary presupposition of our practices. Yet the latter are bereft of any ontological guarantees beyond the constituents of 'our' form of life. Thus the 'correct' ethical self-understanding is neither revealed nor 'given' in any other sense. The self-critical appropriation of our own individual life histories also remains, in a certain sense, a joint construction. From this perspective, what makes our selfhood possible seems to be more a transsubjective than an absolute power. This modest interpretation of the 'founding power' of a linguistically constituted form of life does not, of course, measure up to Kierkegaard's idea that moral obligations owe their binding force to the fact that they are embedded in a religious understanding of ourselves which lends our life meaning.

Max Horkheimer's remark that any attempt to 'salvage an unconditional meaning without God' is 'futile' must also be understood in this metacritical sense.[17] Anyone who agrees with Horkheimer that, following the death of God, any claim to *unconditional* validity must be abandoned faces an unpleasant alternative: either to despair of radical scepticism or to embrace the theological substance of sin and redemption. I do not think that this alternative is inescapable,[18] but the intuition underlying it was clearly so powerful that it left its mark on the most important philosophical works of the twentieth century. In the wake of the convulsions of the First World War, many philosophers were convinced that the nostalgic defeatism concerning reason reflected in Horkheimer's text could be overcome only through a rational translation of the religious notion of a 'God in time'. The point is to translate the Mosaic conception of God into concepts of an impersonal but temporalized Absolute. This is the key to the work of Adorno and Derrida. But is it also the key to that of Heidegger?

Bear with me while I make a suitably brief comparison between Adorno and Heidegger as regards their loyalty to the monotheistic heritage. Whereas the former draws inspiration from the messianic sources of western

Marxism, the latter seems to follow Nietzsche in an attempt to 'retreat' behind the Jewish origins of monotheism and the Platonic origins of metaphysics.

(5)   Negative dialectics can be understood as the working out of an idea which Adorno expresses in the following terms in the final aphorism of *Minima Moralia*:

> the only philosophy which can be responsibly practised in the face of despair is the attempt to contemplate all things as they would present themselves from the standpoint of redemption. Knowledge has no light but that shed on the world by redemption ... Perspectives must be fashioned that displace and estrange the world, reveal it to be, with it rifts and crevices, as indigent and distorted as it will appear one day in the messianic light.[19]

The counterfactual appeal to such perspectives is justified in terms reminiscent of Kierkegaard's famous formula of 'faith': to become aware of one's finitude in a way that does not cut off the human mind from the 'relation to the infinite, to the possible and the transcendent'. Adorno, who knew his Kierkegaard well, also remains true to this self-transcending insight, which proceeds from the despairing defiance of self-assertion at the moment of crisis when he continues:

> the more passionately thought denies its conditionality for the sake of the unconditional, the more unconsciously, and so calamitously, it is delivered up to the world. Even its own impossibility it must at last comprehend for the sake of the possible.[20]

In the closing sentence, however, Adorno retracts the theological allusion and reminds the reader of the inner-worldly context from which he speaks: 'But beside the demand thus placed on thought, the question of the reality or unreality of redemption itself hardly matters.'[21] The moral point of the retracted allusion to God the Redeemer is the methodological 'standpoint' of redemption. Adorno indirectly implies that he remains loyal to the egalitarian–individualistic universalism inscribed in the concept of the *Deus absconditus*. When each of us appears as an irreplaceable individual before the sight of God on the Day of Judgment, to answer for his unique life history, everyone will receive justice in the same way under God's penetrating and merciful gaze. It is this normative substance of monotheism which Adorno wants to hold on to in the disenchanted secular consciousness – and which, if I am not mistaken, gets lost in Heidegger.

To be sure, Kierkegaard's existential analysis of what would be required for a life beyond despair has found no better philosophical expression than in *Being and Time*. But the ontologizing translation of Kierkegaard's modalities of an 'authentic' or ethical life robs Heidegger's conception of the repudiation of the inauthentic of its moral core: 'In the end, Heidegger and Kierkegaard move in opposite directions. Unlike Kierkegaard's ethical life which constitutes a precondition of moral and social responsibility, Heidegger's methodological conception of authenticity is deeply anti-normative.'[22] The empty appeal to a resoluteness devoid of substance anticipates the emptiness of the advent of 'Being' – the uncertain coming of an indeterminate event which is nevertheless invoked as a higher power. Heidegger retains the ontological approach in his later philosophy, when he replaces Kierkegaard's 'God in history' with the history of anonymous being and interprets the defiant self-affirmation of the will 'to want to be oneself' in terms of that single-minded subjectivism which allegedly achieved 'historico-ontological' supremacy through the mentalistic paradigm.

The history of being manifests itself in a contingent series of fateful but overpowering events; it manifests itself in the succession of world-disclosing languages and conceptual frameworks which we owe to the creativity of poets and thinkers. The conversion from a Socratic self-understanding of the ethical self to the awareness of absolute dependence on the mercy and judgment of the Christian redemptive God is replaced by the yet-to-be-accomplished turn, away from the totalizing thinking of the metaphysical tradition and towards the humble subjection to a high power. This inscrutable power, which makes itself felt through its all-consuming absence, demands the devoted obedience of disciples who await attentively the uncertain arrival of foretold tidings. The only information we now possess is the diagnosis of crisis, which is based on the critical reading of the history of metaphysics. From his reading of Nietzsche, Heidegger developed a recommendation on which he based his *Letter on Humanism*: 'We must ... dismiss all the ideas about justice which derive from a Christian, humanist, Enlightenment, bourgeois, and socialist morality.'[23] The assimilation of ethics to ontology led Heidegger in 1946 to answer the basic ethical question with an appeal to the empty ethos of 'fittingness' [or 'propriety': '*Schicklichkeit*']. He instructs his contemporaries to submit to the destiny [or aptitude: *Geschick*] of a higher power – a still absent power, about which we know nothing definite as yet.

The evacuation of all moral content from the temporalized 'being' – apart from an 'obedience' ['*Hörigkeit*'] 'consonant' with it – is the result of strategic theoretical decisions underlying the conception of the history of being. First Heidegger subsumes the monotheistic traditions under the heading of the 'ontotheology' of the history of metaphysics. In the process, the Judeo-Christian tradition also succumbs to the critique of this history. This work of 'destruction' is motivated by the desire to return to archaic beginnings which are supposedly 'more original' and more illuminating than Socrates and Moses/Christ, the two sources of the West which Kierkegaard admires and Nietzsche attacks. This leads Heidegger to speak of 'gods' instead of God in the singular. Let me remind you of the title of the *Spiegel* interview of 31 May 1976: 'Only another (!) god can save us.'

Adorno's critique of the 'thinking of origins' represents the antithesis to this 'incipient thought'.

There is also a 'last god' echoing Nietzsche's 'last man'. His death, according to Heidegger, also marks the end of all 'theistic' traditions. Heidegger's 'remembrance' [*Andenken*'] of being bears no trace of the egalitarian–individualistic universalism inscribed in the monotheistic traditions. In this regard, the fictional dialogue featuring Heidegger which Derrida adds at the end of this book is of great interest. In this dialogue Heidegger encounters 'certain Christian theologians, perhaps the most demanding ...'[24] The scene is conceived in such a way that the theologians try to get Heidegger to reconsider his brusque rejection of the monotheistic traditions. The Christians lead the discussion, but Derrida also mentions messianic Jews and Muslims. Surely, argue the theologians, Heidegger can recognize that his critique of the reifying thinking of ontotheology represents the optimal interpretation of an experience to which the religiously devout expose themselves when they encounter their God in his immediate historical realization, his essence as it manifests itself in history. As one might expect, Derrida's Heidegger responds in a defensive manner to this demand. He insists on the fundamentalist claim of his search for an origin prior to the beginnings of metaphysics and eschatology. Of course, Derrida formulates Heidegger's rejection so carefully that the suspicion of a 'neo-pagan' regression cannot arise among the theologians. The truly striking aspect of this exchange between these improbable partners, however, is that Derrida does not leave the last word to Heidegger but to his intransigent opponents. He allows *them* to reformulate their offer of reconciliation and to lure a recalcitrant Heidegger over to their side with their strategy of embrace. Heidegger is depicted in this dialogue as someone who captures precisely what faith in their 'God in history' means for Jews and Christians: 'Yes, precisely, his interlocutors would reply, that's just what we're saying, at the same crossing of paths ...'[25]

The surprising conclusion shows that Derrida's appropriation of the late Heidegger rests on theological rather than pre-Socratic, on Jewish rather than Greek foundations. His loyalty to Levinas becomes apparent in his tendency to answer the basic ethical question from the perspective of a self-reflexive relation of the ego towards an other, who expresses himself in the voice of a second person. If I am not completely mistaken in this regard, I can formulate the question which I would like to pose to Jacques Derrida as follows: Can Derrida leave the normative connotations of the uncertain advent of an indeterminate event as vague as Heidegger does? If not, what burdens of proof follow from the willingness to render explicit these connotations which are not contingent implications of a particular religious tradition?

Postscript

Although Derrida evaded my question during the meeting in Paris, he responded differently in Fall 2003. At that time I sent Derrida a response which I wanted to give to the corresponding question posed by Eduardo Mendieta in a written interview, in order to avoid misunderstandings. Derrida responded immediately to my fax with a telephone call in which he assured me of his agreement – more unreservedly and spontaneously than I had anticipated – saying that he recently had second thoughts about Heidegger. The subject of this final conversation between us was the following passage from an interview on 'War and Peace':[26]

On May 31, you and Derrida published a manifesto of sorts under the title: 'February 15, or: What Binds Europeans. A Plea for a Common Foreign Policy – Beginning with Core Europe'. In a preliminary remark, Derrida explains that he is co-signing the article which you wrote. How is it that two intellectual heavyweights who for the past two decades have eyed each other suspiciously across the Rhine – while, as some maintain, talking past each other – could suddenly agree to co-publish such an important document? Is it simply 'politics', or is the text you co-signed also a 'philosophical gesture'? An amnesty, a truce, a reconciliation, a philosophical gift?

I have no idea how Derrida would answer your question. For my taste, your formulations smack of overstatement. First, it is, of course, a political statement, one on which Derrida and I happen to agree – as has often occurred in recent years, by the way. After the formal conclusion of the Iraq War, when many people feared a general prostration of the 'unwilling' governments before Bush, I sent a letter to Derrida – as well as to Eco, Muschg, Rorty, Savater, and Vattimo – inviting them to participate in a joint initiative. (Paul Ricoeur was the only one who declined for political reasons; Eric Hobsbawm and Harry Mulisch could not participate for personal reasons.) Derrida was not able to write an article of his own either, because he had to undergo unpleasant medical tests at the time. However, Derrida very much wanted to participate in the initiative and suggested the procedure which we then followed. I was pleased about this. We had last met in New York after September 11. We had already resumed our philosophical conversation some years earlier in Evanston, Paris, and Frankfurt. So there was no need for a grand gesture.

Derrida, for his part, gave a very subtle lecture in the Paulskirche in Frankfurt on receiving the Adorno Prize, which revealed the intellectual affinity between these two thinkers in an impressive way. Such a gesture does not leave one unmoved. Moreover, aside from all political questions, what unites me with Derrida is the philosophical reference to an author like Kant. Admittedly we part ways over the later Heidegger – even though we are roughly the same age, our lives have followed very different paths. Derrida assimilates Heidegger's ideas from the

Jewish-inspired standpoint of a Levinas. I encounter Heidegger as a philosopher who failed as a citizen, in 1933 and especially after 1945. But he is suspect for me even as a philosopher because, during the 1930s, he interpreted Nietzsche precisely in the neo-pagan fashion then in vogue. Unlike Derrida, whose reading of '*Andenken*' [lit. 'remembrance'] accords with the spirit of the monotheistic tradition, I regard Heidegger's botched '*Seinsdenken*' [lit. 'thinking of being'] as a leveling of the epochal threshold in the history of consciousness which Jaspers called the 'Axial Age'. On my understanding, Heidegger betrayed that caesura which is marked, in different ways, by the prophetic awakening of Mount Sinai and by the philosophical enlightenment of a Socrates.

Insofar as Derrida and I understand each other's respective background motives, an interpretive difference need not necessarily mean a difference over the thing interpreted. At any rate, 'truce' and 'reconciliation' are not the right terms for a congenial, open-minded exchange.

3
Ronald Dworkin – A Maverick among Legal Scholars*

Our first meeting was in September 1983, during sit-in demonstrations to protest against the German government's decision to station missiles in Mutlangen and elsewhere. Peter Glotz, at the time Secretary General of the German Social Democratic Party, had organized a debate on civil disobedience in Bonn. Following various committed lectures, Heinrich Böll came up to me and pointed out an American professor who had been flown in from London to lend the event argumentative weight, rhetoric brilliance, and international flair, and he asked full of curiosity: 'Who exactly is that?' Back then, a law professor who justified trained civil disobedience was a rarity. And Ronald Dworkin has remained an exceptional figure. He is a maverick both among legal scholars and among philosophers; he enjoys high standing among the public intellectuals of his country; and he is a brilliant political speaker. With somewhat less talent, contrariness, and ingeniousness, I suspect that he would have long since become a Supreme Court justice in Washington. This evening I will try to answer Heinrich Böll's question.

***

*Speech held in honor of Ronal Dworkin on his receiving the Niklas Luhmann Prize on 15 December 2006.

If you open Ronald Dworkin's book *Justice in Robes*, which has just come out, at the very beginning you will find a story about a legendary figure among America's famous judges:

> When Oliver Holmes was an Associate Justice of the Supreme Court he gave the young Learned Hand [who was to become Dworkin's teacher] a lift in his carriage as Holmes made his way to the Court. Hand got out at his destination, waved after the departing carriage, and called out merrily, 'Do justice, Justice!' Holmes ordered the driver to stop the cab and turn around, rode back to the astonished Hand and said, leaning out of the window: 'That's not my job.' Then the carriage turned and departed, taking Holmes back to his job of allegedly not doing justice.

Dworkin uses this anecdote to illustrate a question that has preoccupied him his entire life: What influence may, or even should, a judge's moral convictions have on his rulings?

Needless to say, a legal scholar knows that law and justice are two very different things. But may the judge in robes completely ignore the internal relation between law and justice? Indeed, could he do so even if he wanted to? At this point a methodological distinction is important, which I can explain by referring to the famous social theorist in whose name Ronald Dworkin is being honored here tonight.

Niklas Luhmann describes the legal system from the distance of a sociological observer, and includes the self-description of the lawyer and the legal theorist in his own detached description. Dworkin, by contrast, develops his theory of law from the perspective of the participants who, in cases of conflict, seek and pass judgments in accordance with what the law demands. Dworkin calls the judge whom he observes at work 'Hercules', because he who passes judgment, too, continues to search for the single right answer in each case. In contrast to Luhmann's ecumenical embrace of all participants, Dworkin insists that the sociologist also has to understand the *point* of the practice of adjudication from the standpoint of a virtual participant before withdrawing to the objectifying stance of the observer. Without this prior hermeneutic view, even the legal code of what is just and unjust would remain a black box for the sociologist. Here the question is: Who can embrace whom – the sociologist the legal philosopher, or vice versa?

Interestingly enough, more turns on this question than merely a methodological choice between the approaches of the one or the other discipline. The answer hinges instead on a long-standing dispute among legal scholars over which concept of law is the correct one: Can the law be construed as a morally neutral set of norms? Because Ronald Dworkin and Niklas Luhmann, as the legal scholars they are by training, offer contrary answers to this question, they set off in opposite directions starting from their home discipline. Both develop wide-ranging and influential theories of law and politics, the one as a social scientist, the other as a philosopher. In the process they drift ever further apart, because their paths bifurcated at the very beginning.

***

The issue concerns their respective positions on the tradition of legal positivism, which Luhmann wants to continue, but which Dworkin rejects. Dworkin began his career with a provocative critique of H. L. A. Hart, whom he was, incidentally, to succeed in the Chair of Jurisprudence at Oxford. He elaborated on this critique in 1977, in his first major work, *Taking Rights Seriously*, and even in his most recent publication he has defended his hypothesis against the responses which were found among Hart's unpublished writings. Legal positivism takes into account the changeability of modern law and the intrinsic structure of the legal medium. However, the price it pays for emphasizing the formal properties of compulsory legal norms already highlighted by Kant is an abstract division between law and morality. Dworkin has nothing against an appropriate distinction between the two types of norms, but he does object to the moral neutralization of law.

As a student at Harvard, Dworkin came into contact with the ideas which John Rawls subsequently published in his *Theory of Justice* (1971). That book marked a caesura. Afterwards even in analytical philosophy the strict division between the evaluative content of moral judgments and the supposedly value-free meta-ethical study of these judgments was no longer tenable. Since then, mainstream Anglo-American philosophy takes it for granted again that moral judgments have a cognitive content, and hence can be criticized and justified. Just as important was the method of Kantian constructivism through which Rawls triggered the revolution in the hitherto dominant empiricist approach. Following this lead, Dworkin was able to ignite the revolutionary spark in legal theory as well, without falling back into the sterile dispute between positivism and classical natural law. In order to demonstrate the moral substance of law in the process of its application, one now only needed to adopt the parsimonious moral point of view from which we owe everybody 'equal respect and concern'.

It goes without saying that the judge is bound by the facts of the established legal order as this is enacted by the political legislators and interpreted by the courts. For without legal certainty, that is, without a certain degree of predictability in legal decision-making, the law would not be able to perform its function of coordinating actions and stabilizing behavioral expectations. On the other hand, a judge cannot take his cue from binding statutes and precedents alone; he must also take into account standards which are convincing – also for himself – in the present. The administration of justice would collapse without the intersubjectively shared presupposition that a case before the courts has a good chance of being decided 'correctly'. How can the judge bring this reference to moral convictions in the present into harmony with the backward-looking reference to the body of established law? Hercules must not allow himself to be disconcerted in his search for the single right answer; he must have confidence in his ability to disclose, from the perspective of each individual case, the legal order as an integrated but flexible whole of principles and rules. The correct solution for a case at hand can be discovered only as the result of a constructive achievement, because the relevant principles and rules are brought into the correct ranking only through a context-sensitive and case-specific mode of argument.

In his book *Law's Empire* published in 1986, Dworkin develops this ingenious idea of a constructive interpretation of law guided by principles under the ambiguous heading of 'integrity'. Here Dworkin not only wants to bring hermeneutic insights to bear against a false algorithmic model of the application of law. He is not only concerned with a holistic view of the coherence of the legal order that judges must create *in casu*. One can speak of the 'integrity' of a legal order only when the moral contents of the legal principles cohere in such a way that the legality of each individual decision can derive a surplus of moral legitimacy from the fit between the parts and the whole.[1] That is the case wherever rights are 'taken seriously', namely in the constitutional state which enacts human rights as positive basic rights. For human rights cast moral content in the mould of individual rights, in which form moral content acquires the status of enforceable law. And through these channels the moral content then permeates and suffuses the legal order as a whole.

This position compels Dworkin to wage a battle on two fronts. He opposes not only the legal positivists, who neutralize the moral substance of law, but also the legal realists, who assimilate law to politics and use it as an additional instrument to shape the future. Dworkin

41

defends the inherent normative thrust of the legal medium against attempts to reduce law to the instrumental role of an organizational arm of state power. Anyone who takes rights seriously must not weigh them up against undesirable consequences and simply subordinate the 'conditional programs' (in Luhmann's terms) to political goals. Given the inflationary talk of 'legal assets' ['*Rechtsgüter*'], Dworkin insists on the categorical difference between norms and policy goals. If rights are to preserve the deontological meaning of a protective cover for the individual citizen against the pull of a utilitarian assessment of consequences, they must retain sufficient force to out-trump collective goals on a regular basis.

***

Dworkin's distinctive legal theory is, of course, only the starting point for a comprehensive oeuvre which has its roots in ethics and extends to political philosophy and even branches out into epistemological issues. To regard Dworkin the philosopher as a legal theorist would be like mistaking Luhmann the social theorist for a sociologist of law. Dworkin's early essay on liberalism, published in 1978,[2] already reveals the larger philosophical picture. From the outset, Dworkin wanted to set political and legal philosophy on a broader footing. He develops the basic concepts and procedures of the constitutional state out of the substance, and in the combative spirit, of an ethical liberalism. This vision stands and falls with a preferred conception of the good life and of a specific form of life.

The Aristotelian in Ronald Dworkin does not shy away from offering anthropological arguments for the just society. The correct 'image of man' bears the aesthetic and expressive traits of a creative individual who feels the obligation to make something productive of his or her life. Dworkin starts from the insight that we are responsible for shaping our lives. He does not leave the last word to Kant. At the Last Judgment we will not be first called upon to account for the injuries we inflicted on others but for the opportunities we missed in failing to lead a successful life of our own.[3] Respect for others is grounded in a generalized duty to oneself: we not only desire that our life should be successful, we are also obliged to make something out of it. And from this moral responsibility for realizing the potential implicit in one's own life history Dworkin wants to derive a political duty to take account of the competing responsibilities that others have for realizing the objective value of their lives.[4]

This primacy of the individual's ethical freedom over the moral–political liberty of the citizen is the key to understanding the interesting difference between Rawls's and Dworkin's respective concepts of distributive justice. As a social democrat, Rawls believes that in a capitalist society only that level of social inequality is legitimate which even the most disadvantaged members of society would also accept as being in their interest. In his ambitious book *Sovereign Equality* (2000), by contrast, Dworkin develops a social–liberal theory of distributive justice with a focus on the priority of individual liberties. Because the liberty of private persons is granted pride of place, each person bears the risk for the choice of the life he or she would like to lead. Equal opportunity is assured by the fact that all participants start out with the same resources, and they strike a balance between more and less cost-intensive life plans through a kind of auction. The principle of equal resources calls for compensatory benefits for the deficits and handicaps which we suffer through no fault of our own, because of unfavorable circumstances or because of genetic makeup.

The auction model represents a fictive initial state in which everybody decides on the risks to take for their preferred way of life. The basic idea is that the price people should pay for the life they wish to enjoy should be measured in terms of what others have to give up so that they can do so. Instead of an equality of outcomes, justice only requires that each person should have the

43

same resources at his or her disposal *at the outset*. This extremely sophisticated experimental design has garnered much admiration among experts.

***

A speech about Ronald Dworkin the philosopher and legal theorist still misses a key feature of this vibrant personality. I am thinking of the alertness of an intellectual who has written eloquent commentaries and expert opinions for many decades, addressing topical issues in the pages of the *New York Review of Books* and of the most prominent law reviews of the country. Dworkin's unique blend of argumentative acuity and rhetorical elegance stems no doubt from his early training as a lawyer who learned to represent his client's cause before the court. As a citizen and as an intellectual, Dworkin no longer has any clients, of course, but he acts on his own initiative, intervening in debates even when there is little prospect of political success.

In America, since the 1960s, there has scarcely been a single public political controversy of note which has not prompted Dworkin to challenge his political opponents before the forum of reasoned debate. It might be a question of affirmative action or abortion, pornography and free speech, hate speech or assisted suicide, dubious candidacies for the Supreme Court or eccentric verdicts of the same – for example when the Court, as in *Gore v. Bush*, strained the constitution instead of protecting it. In this role, Dworkin the lawyer is supported by the culture of a country in which political issues are transformed into hard cases before the courts.

However, a link to the practice of the committed intellectual is already forged by the theory of the lawyer and philosopher when it discerns, in the fragments of existing law, a system of rights which insists on an ever more exhaustive implementation. The sorry facts of the existing condition of law already betray the aspiration to a properly

44

understood rule of law. This is the sense in which Dworkin speaks of the aspirational concept of law. This is an expression of a very American form of patriotism, whose moving thrust another US philosopher, Richard Rorty, has couched in a concept beyond suspicion when he spoke of 'achieving our country'. Ronald Dworkin's most recent book provides moving testimony to this Brechtian impulse to improve his own country.[5]

This short treatise addresses the question 'Is Democracy Possible Here?' and begins with the admission that 'American politics is in an appalling state'. It begins in this way only because it is intended to show a way out of the country's frightening political polarization between the camps of the religious right and a marginalized liberalism. Though Dworkin does not, of course, deny his advocacy of the liberal cause, in defending it he adopts the role of a moderator, who patiently lets both sides say their piece first, before going on to remind them of the values they share as American citizens.

Dworkin does not shy away from any controversy. He dauntlessly addresses Guantanamo and the denial of prisoners' basic legal rights, the dangers of terrorism, and the torture practices euphemistically termed 'coercive interrogation'; he discusses the security interests of the state, the curtailments of the civil rights of the individual, the death penalty, and the utilitarian hollowing out of criminal law; he writes about religious fundamentalism and the neutrality of the state, about homosexual marriage and the issue, posed by creationism, of the relation between biblical faith and scientific authority; he even comments on neoliberal economic policies and on the question of social justice, on the welfare state as a precondition for democratic legitimation, and on the destruction of the political public sphere by the media power of private corporations. But what sets Dworkin's argumentation apart on this occasion is the fact that, as a patriot, he evokes the common ground of a shared political culture across these deep divisions among citizens. Here we encounter the voice of a man appealing to his political opponents in the spirit of 'We Americans', lest they forget the better part of their national values.

Since I am aware of how susceptible I am to polemics in such overwrought situations, I would like to express my admiration for the democratic spirit of this intervention, which is intended to foster consensus and to ensure that the thread of discursive argument is not severed, even with extreme opponents. Blind trust in the capacity of one's own political culture to resist being torn asunder is obviously not without its dangers; but where this faith is justified, it is an expression of a more mature democratic tradition.

Part II
Europe, the Faltering Project

4
An Avantgardistic Instinct for Relevances: The Role of the Intellectual and the European Cause*

When the director of the Karl Renner Institute sent me the welcome news that the jury wished to award me this year's Bruno Kreisky Prize, I had occasion to reflect not only on my perplexing good fortune in meeting with so much undeserved recognition, after decades of controversy allied to a rather controversial reputation. In addition, the names of those two historical figures who do so much honor to the eventful history of the Austrian republic led me to consider for the first time my relation to the Viennese social democrats. It's not that the relation was a political one. However, the names of Karl Renner and Bruno Kreisky remind me of the intellectual inspiration which I owe to an important theoretical tradition. I would like to take this opportunity to acknowledge a debt of gratitude to Austro-Marxism for two crucial intellectual impulses.

Debt to Austro-Marxism

I arrived in the unfamiliar surroundings of the Frankfurt Institute for Social Research in 1956, having completed a fairly conventional philosophical education. In prepara-

*Acceptance speech on receiving the Bruno Kreisky Prize at the University of Vienna on 9 March 2006.

tion for an empirical study, I had to familiarize myself with the literature on democracy and on the constitutional state, which at the time was still the exclusive preserve of legal scholars. Although I found the debates between the major constitutional lawyers of the Weimar Republic absorbing, it was difficult for me to relate the normative concepts of jurisprudence to the social theory in terms of which I was trying to make sense of contemporary politics. One book, in particular, opened my eyes to the relation between political economy and law. This book, published in 1929 under the unwieldy title *Die Rechtsinstitute des Privatrechts und ihre soziale Funktion*,[1] drew upon studies conducted by the young Karl Renner around the turn of the century, while he was working as a librarian in the Reichsrat, the Austrian parliament.[2]

This is how I came into contact with writings of the Austro-Marxists in which I found three things I missed as Adorno's assistant in Frankfurt. The first was the fact that they treated the connection between theory and political practice as a matter of course. Second, there was the unabashed opening of Marxist social theory to insights from academic research (a mindset that Horkheimer and Adorno had abandoned again, since their *Dialectic of Enlightenment*). And, third and most importantly, there was their unconditional identification with the achievements of the constitutional state, while upholding radical reformist aims which went far beyond the status quo.

In my development from Hegelian Marxism to a form of Kantian pragmatism in the late 1960s, the book of another Austro-Marxist – Max Adler's late work, which appeared in 1936 under the title *Das Rätsel der Gesellschaft* – served as a comparably far-reaching stimulus.[3] In introducing the idea of a 'social a priori', Adler reminds us not only that our ego-consciousness and our knowledge of the world are socially constituted but also that, conversely, social relations are constructed on the basis of acts of cognition. But this implies that society is itself founded on the facticity [*Faktizität*] of validity claims which we raise through our communicative utterances. In this way Adler argues, not unlike the late Husserl, that a relation to the truth of statements and to the rightness of norms is imminent in society itself.[4]

In spite of their scientific ambitions, Otto Bauer, Rudolf Hilferding, Karl Renner, and Max Adler saw themselves as party intellectuals who submitted to tactical and organizational discipline when the occasion demanded. As democrats, however, they had a completely different conception of the role of the party from Lukács's Leninist conception in *History and Class Consciousness*. Be that as it may, the party intellectual belongs to the historical milieu of left-wing ideological parties. This type of thinker was no longer possible in the West after 1945. Like Willy Brandt, Bruno Kreisky too returned from Scandinavia a changed man. To these social democrats returning from emigration we also owe the pacification of class society through the welfare state and its transformation into a civil society.

The figure of the contemporary intellectual contrasts sharply with this background. The intellectuals who came to prominence after 1945, such as Camus and Sartre, Adorno and Marcuse, Max Frisch and Heinrich Böll, were closer to the older model of the committed writers and professors who were not bound to any political party. Given a suitable occasion, they could be provoked, without being invited and thus without instruction or prior agreement, into putting their expertise to public use beyond the limits of their profession. Without a claim to an elite status, they had to derive their legitimation solely from their role as democratic citizens.

Intellectuals and their Public

The roots of this egalitarian self-understanding in Germany extend back to the first generation after Goethe and Hegel. The restive literati and private lecturers from the circle of Young Germany and of the Left Hegelians nurtured both the image of free-floating, spontaneous, intensely polemical, often maudlin, and unpredictable intellectuals and the prejudices against them which persist to this day. It is no accident that the generation of Feuerbach, Heine, and Börne, of Bruno Bauer, Max Stirner, and Julius Fröbel, of Marx, Engels, and Kierkegaard appeared on the scene before 1848, when parliamentarianism and the mass press were emerging under the auspices of early liberalism.

During this incubation period, as the virus of the French Revolution was spreading throughout Europe, the constellation in which the figure of the modern intellectual would find its place was already beginning to take shape. When intellectuals influence the formation of opinions through rhetorically pointed arguments, they depend on a responsive, alert, and informed public. They need a more or less liberal-minded public and must rely on a halfway functioning constitutional state, for the simple reason that they appeal to universalistic values in struggles for suppressed truths or withheld rights. They belong to a world in which politics is not synonymous with state action; their world is a political culture of contestation in which the communicative freedoms of the citizens can be set free and mobilized.

It is easy to sketch the ideal type of an intellectual who seeks out important issues, proposes fruitful hypotheses, and broadens the spectrum of relevant arguments in an attempt to improve the lamentable level of public debates. On the other hand, I should not gloss over the favorite activity of intellectuals, namely their eagerness to join in the ritual lament over the decline of 'the' intellectual. I must confess that I am not completely free from this impulse myself.

How we miss the grand performances and manifestos of the Group 47, the interventions of Alexander Mitscherlich and Helmuth Gollwitzer, the political stances of Michel Foucault, Jacques Derrida, and Pierre Bourdieu, the combative texts of Erich Fried and Günter Grass! Is it really Grass's fault that his voice mostly meets with indifference today? Or is our media society once again undergoing a structural transformation of the public sphere which is inimical to intellectuals of the classical type?

On the one hand, the recalibration of communication from print and the press to television and the Internet has led to an unexpected expansion of the public sphere of the media and to an unparalleled expansion of communications networks. The public sphere in which intellectuals moved like fish in water has become more inclusive, and the exchanges more intense than ever before. On the other hand, the intellectuals seem to be choking on this life-sustaining element like on an overdose. The blessing seems to be turning into a curse. In my view this is because the public sphere is becoming more informal and the corresponding roles are becoming blurred.

Internet use has led to an expansion and fragmentation of communications networks. Thus, although the Internet has a subversive effect on public spheres under authoritarian regimes, at the same time the horizontal and informal networking of communications diminishes the achievements of traditional public spheres. For the latter pool the attention of an anonymous and dispersed public within political communities for selected messages, so that the citizens can address the same critically filtered issues and contributions at the same time. The price for the welcome increase in egalitarianism due to the Internet is a decentering of the modes of access to unedited inputs. In this medium, the contributions of intellectuals can no longer constitute a focal point.

However, the assertion that the electronic revolution is destroying the stage for the elitist performances of conceited intellectuals would be premature. For, if anything, television, which essentially operates within the national public arenas, has enlarged the stage for the press, magazines, and literature. However, television has also transformed this stage. It has to present its message in images and has accelerated the 'iconic turn' from word to image. This relative demotion also entails a shift in importance between

53

two different functions of the public sphere. Because television is a medium which makes things visible, it confers celebrity in the form of fame on those who make public appearances. Whatever else they may contribute to the content of the program, those who appear before the camera are also presenting themselves. As a result, in casual encounters the viewers remember that they have seen the face before. Even in the case of programs with a discursive content, television induces the participants to engage in self-promotion, as in the numerous talk shows. This element of self-promotion inevitably transforms the judging public – which takes part, before the television, in debates over issues of general interest – into a viewing public as well.

It is not as though this does not feed the pathological vanity of intellectuals, many of whom have allowed themselves to be corrupted by the inducement of the medium to self-promotion, at the cost of their reputations. For the good reputation of an intellectual, assuming she has one, is not based primarily on celebrity or fame, but on a standing which has to be acquired in her own field, whether as a writer or as a physicist, at any rate in some specialist field, before she makes a public use of her knowledge and reputation. When she contributes arguments to a debate, she must address a public composed, not of viewers, but of potential speakers and addressees who are able to offer each other justifications. This is, ideally, a matter of exchanging reasons, not of hogging the limelight through a carefully staged performance.

Perhaps this is why the groups of politicians, experts, and journalists invited by one of those fabulous talk-show hostesses do not leave any room to be filled by an intellectual. We don't miss the intellectual because her role is already performed better by the other participants.

The blurring of the boundaries between discourse and self-promotion leads to a loss of differentiation and to an assimilation of the roles which the now old-fashioned intellectual had once to keep apart. She was not supposed to use the influence she had acquired through her words to gain power, and thus to confuse 'influence' with 'power'. But, in the present-day talk-show landscape, what could still set her apart from politicians who have long used the television as a stage for an intellectual contest over the monopoly of influential issues and concepts? The intellectual was not in demand as an expert. She was supposed to have the courage to take normative stances and the imagination to adopt novel perspectives without losing an awareness of her own fallibility. But what could still set her apart from the experts, who have learnt long ago how to offer opinionated interpretations of their findings in debates with opposing experts?

What is ultimately supposed to distinguish intellectuals from clever journalists is less the mode of presentation than the privilege of having to deal with public issues only as a sideline. They are supposed to speak out only when current events are threatening to spin out of control – but then promptly, as an early warning system.

With this we come to the sole ability which could still set intellectuals apart today, namely an avantgardistic instinct for relevances. They have to be able to get worked up about critical developments while others are still absorbed in business as usual. This calls for quite unheroic virtues:

- a mistrustful sensitivity to damage to the normative infrastructure of the polity;
- the anxious anticipation of threats to the mental resources of the shared political form of life;
- the sense for what is lacking and 'could be otherwise';
- a spark of imagination in conceiving of alternatives;
- and a modicum of the courage required for polarizing, provoking, and pamphleteering.

That is – and always has been – more easily said than done. The intellectual should have the ability to get worked up – and yet should have sufficient political judgment not to overreact. What their critics – from Max Weber and Schumpeter to Gehlen and Schelsky – reproach them

55

with is the persistent accusation of 'sterile enthusiasm' and 'alarmism'. They should not let themselves be intimidated by this reproach. Even though Sartre was the more influential intellectual than Aron, he was more often mistaken in his political judgments. To be sure, the instinct for what is relevant can go terribly wrong. For example, a historian who calls for the reintroduction of the 'political cult of the dead' which Germany turned its back on after 1945 can't fail to make a fool of himself. Clearly the man hasn't any notion of the mental core of fascism.

The Future of Europe

Others find my main current preoccupation, the future of Europe, abstract and boring. Why should we get worked up about such a tame issue? My answer is simple: if we don't succeed in making the key question of the *finalité* – the ultimate goal – of European unification into the topic of a European-wide referendum by the time the next European election comes around in 2009, then the neoliberal orthodoxy will have decided the future of the European Union.

We can't afford to avoid this thorny issue for the sake of a shabby peace and to muddle through with the usual compromises. For that would be to give free rein to the dynamics of the unbridled markets and to stand by while even the existing regulatory power of the European Union is unraveled in favor of a diffusely enlarged European free trade zone. For the first time in the process of European unification, we face the danger of a regression behind the stage of integration already achieved. What bothers me is the paralysis following the failure of the two constitutional referenda in France and the Netherlands. A nondecision in this situation is a decision of great moment.

I would like to have discussed this issue in the country which currently holds the presidency of the European Council, had I not been invited to address you on the role of the intellectual. As it turns out, the one issue has led me to the other. The single problem of the inadequate decision-making power of the European Union involves three urgent and intertwined problems:

1 Global economic conditions, which have been transformed under the pressure of globalization, today prevent the nation–state from drawing upon the taxation revenues they need in order to meet the established social welfare claims and, more generally, the demand for collective goods and public services to a sufficient extent. Other challenges, such as the demographic trends and the rising levels of immigration, are aggravating the situation. The only way out is to recuperate the lost political regulatory power at the supranational level. Without convergent tax rates and without the prospect of harmonizing economic and social policy in the medium term, we leave the fate of the European social model in the hands of others.

2 The return to a reckless, hegemonic power politics, the clash of the West with the Islamic world, the collapse of state structures in other parts of the world, the long-term social impacts of colonialism, and the immediate political consequences of unsuccessful decolonization – all of these indicators point to an extremely precarious global situation. Only a European Union with an effective foreign policy, which assumes global political responsibilities alongside the United States, China, India, and Japan, could promote an alternative to the dominant Washington Consensus within the existing global economic institutions and, most importantly, could lend impetus to the long-overdue reforms of the United Nations which are currently being blocked by the United States, though they can be achieved only with its support.

3 The split within the West which has become apparent since the Iraq War is also rooted in a cultural

conflict [*Kulturkampf*], which is splitting the American nation itself into two almost equal camps. This mental shift is leading to a loosening of the normative standards which used to inform government policy. The closest allies of the United States cannot remain indifferent to this development. In critical cases involving joint action, in particular, we must free ourselves from our dependence on the senior partner. For this reason, too, the European Union needs an army of its own. Until now, the Europeans have had to follow the directives and rules of the American supreme command during NATO operations. Now, in conducting joint operations, we have to gain the leeway to respect our own notions of international law, the prohibition of torture, and the law governing war crimes.

This is why, in my view, Europe must face up to a reform process which would not only confer effective decision-making procedures on the Union but also its own foreign minister, a directly elected president, and a financial basis of its own. These requirements could be made the topic of a referendum, to be linked with the next elections to the European Parliament. The proposal would be deemed accepted if it succeeded in winning the 'double majority' of the states and of the votes of the citizens. At the same time, the referendum would be binding only on those member states in which a majority of the citizens voted for the reform. With this Europe would abandon the convoy model, in which the slowest vehicle determines the speed. Even in a Europe of core and periphery, the countries which initially prefer to remain on the sidelines would, of course, have the option of joining the centre at any time.

In making these proposals I find myself in agreement with the Belgian Prime Minister Guy Verhofstadt, who published a manifesto entitled *The United States of Europe* in 2006.[5] As this example shows, politicians who are a step ahead can drag intellectuals along behind them.

5
What is Meant by a 'Post-Secular Society'? A Discussion on Islam in Europe*

A '*post*-secular' society must at some point have been in a 'secular' condition. Thus this controversial term is only applicable to the affluent societies of Europe or to countries such as Canada, Australia, and New Zealand, where people's religious ties have steadily loosened, and quite dramatically so since the end of the Second World War. In these regions, the awareness of belonging to a secularized society had become more or less universal. However, the religious habits and convictions of the local populations, as measured by the usual sociological indicators, have by no means changed sufficiently in the meantime that we would be justified in describing these societies as 'post-secular'. In Germany even the trends towards new, de-institutionalized forms of religiosity and spirituality cannot offset the tangible losses suffered by the major religious communities.[1]

1 Revisiting the Sociological Debate on Secularization

Nevertheless global changes and the conflicts flaring up all around us in connection with religious issues inspire doubts as to whether the relevance of religion has actually

*This text is based on a lecture delivered on 15 March 2007 at the Nexus Institute of the University of Tilburg in the Netherlands.

waned. Ever fewer sociologists support the long unchal-
lenged hypothesis that there is close connection between
social modernization and the secularization of the population.[2] The hypothesis rests on three considerations which
are at first sight plausible:

First, progress in science and technology promotes an
anthropocentric understanding of the 'disenchanted' world,
because the totality of empirical states and events can be
explained in causal terms; and a scientifically enlightened
mind cannot be easily reconciled with theocentric and
metaphysical worldviews. Second, with the functional
differentiation of social subsystems, the churches and other
religious organizations lose their control over law, politics,
public welfare, culture, education, and science; they confine
themselves to their proper function of administering the
means of salvation, they make the exercise of religion into a
predominantly private matter, and they suffer a general loss
in public influence and relevance. Finally, the development
from agrarian to industrial and post-industrial societies
leads to higher levels of welfare and increased social security; and with the easing of everyday risks and growing
existential security, individuals have less need of a practice
that promises to cope with uncontrolled contingencies
through faith in a 'higher' or cosmic power.

Although the secularization hypothesis seems to be
confirmed by developments in the affluent European societies, it has been a matter of controversy among the expert
community of sociologists for the past two decades or
more.[3] In the wake of the not unfounded criticism of a
narrow Eurocentric perspective, there is now even talk of
the 'end of secularization theory'.[4] The United States,
which, notwithstanding the undiminished vibrancy of its
religious communities and its consistently high numbers of
religiously committed and active citizens, remains the
spearhead of modernization, was long regarded as the great
exception to the secularizing trend. Yet, in the light of the
globally extended perspective on other cultures and world
religions, it appears today more like the normal case.

From this revisionist point of view, the European development, which, with its occidental rationalism, was supposed to serve as a model for the rest of the world, is actually the exception or deviant path [*Sonderweg*] rather than the norm.[5] Three overlapping phenomena, more than anything else, converge to create the impression of a worldwide 'resurgence of religion': (a) the missionary expansion of the major world religions; (b) their fundamentalist radicalization; and (c) the political instrumentalization of their inherent potential for violence.

(a) First, a sign of vibrancy is the fact that orthodox, or at any rate conservative, groups within the established religious organizations and churches are everywhere on the advance. This holds as much for Hinduism and Buddhism as it does for the three monotheistic religions. Most striking of all is the regional spread of these established religions in Africa and in the East and Southeast Asian countries. The missionary successes apparently depend also on the flexibility of the corresponding forms of organization. The transnational and multicultural Roman Catholic church is adapting better to the globalizing trend than the nationally organized Protestant churches, which are the principal losers. Most dynamic of all are the decentralized networks of Islam (above all in sub-Saharan Africa) and the Evangelicals (especially in Latin America). What sets them apart is an ecstatic form of religiosity inspired by charismatic leaders.

(b) The fastest growing religious movements, such as the Pentecostals and the radical Muslims, can be most readily described as 'fundamentalist'. They combat the modern world or they withdraw from it. Their forms of worship combine spiritualism and adventism with rigid moral conceptions and literal

61

adherence to holy scripture. By contrast, the 'new religious movements' which have mushroomed since the 1970s are marked more by a 'Californian' syncretism, although they share with the Evangelicals a de-institutionalized form of religious observance. In Japan approximately 400 such sects have arisen, combining elements of Buddhism and popular religion with pseudoscientific and esoteric doctrines. In the People's Republic of China the political repression of the Falun Gong sect has highlighted the large number of 'new religions', whose followers are thought to number as many as eighty million.[6]

(c) The mullah regime in Iran and the worldwide Islamic terrorism are only the most spectacular examples of a political unleashing of the potential for violence inherent in religion. Often smoldering conflicts with profane origins first become ignited when they are coded in religious terms. This holds for the 'desecularization' of the Middle East conflict as much as for the politics of Hindu nationalism and the enduring conflict between India and Pakistan,[7] or for the mobilization of the religious right in the United States before and during the invasion of Iraq.

2 The Descriptive Account of a 'Post-Secular Society' and the Normative Issue of how Citizens of such a Society Should Understand Themselves

Here I cannot discuss in detail the controversy among sociologists concerning the supposed *Sonderweg* of the secularized societies of Europe in the midst of a religiously mobilized world society. My impression is that the data collected globally still provide surprisingly robust support for the defenders of the secularization thesis.[8] In my view, the weakness of the theory of secularization

resides instead in rash inferences which betray an impre-
cise use of the concepts of 'secularization' and 'modernization'. It remains true that, in the course of the
differentiation of functional social systems, churches and
religious communities increasingly confined themselves to
their core function of pastoral care and had to renounce
their wide-ranging competencies in other social domains.
At the same time, the practice of faith also assumed more
personal or subjective forms. A correlation exists between
the functional specification of the religious system and the
individualization of religious practice.

However, as José Casanova correctly points out, the loss
of function and the trend towards individualization do not
necessarily lead to a loss in the *influence and relevance* of
religion, either in the public arena and culture of any
single society or in the personal conduct of life.[9] Quite
apart from their weight in numbers, religious communities can still claim a 'seat' even in the life of societies
where secularization is far advanced. Today the description 'post-secular society' can be applied to public consciousness in Europe in so far as for the time being it
has to 'adjust itself to the continued existence of religious
communities in an increasingly secularized environment'.[10] The revised reading of the secularization hypothesis relates less to its substance and more to the
predictions concerning the future role of 'religion'.

The new description of modern societies as 'post-
secular' refers to a *change in consciousness* which I attribute primarily to three phenomena:

(a)   First, the media-generated perception of the global
conflicts which are often presented as hinging on religious
strife transforms public consciousness. Most European
citizens do not even need obtrusive fundamentalist movements and the fear of religiously-defined terrorism in order
to become aware of the relativity of their secular mentality
on a global scale. This circumstance shakes the secular*istic*
confidence that religion *is destined to disappear* and inocu-

63

lates the secular understanding of the world against triumphalism. The awareness of living in a secular society is no
longer bound up with the *certainty* that cultural and social
modernization can advance only at the cost of the public
influence and personal relevance of religion.

(b)   Second, the influence of religion is increasing not only
worldwide, but also within national public spheres. Here I
am not thinking primarily of skillful public relations on the
part of the churches, but of the fact that religious organizations are increasingly assuming the role of 'communities of
interpretation' within the public arena of secular societies.[11] They can influence the formation of public opinion
and will by making relevant contributions, whether convincing or objectionable, on key issues. Our pluralist societies   provide   a   responsive   sounding   board   for   such
interventions because they are increasingly split over value
conflicts in need of political regulation. Whether it be the
dispute over the legalization of abortion or over voluntary
euthanasia, over bioethical issues in reproductive medicine
or over questions of animal protection and climate change
– in these and similar cases the key premises are so opaque
that it is by no means settled from the outset which party
can draw on the more convincing moral intuitions.
   Incidentally, the visibility and vibrancy of foreign religious communities also enhance the influence of the
established churches and congregations. The Muslims
next door, if I may take an example of relevance for both
the Netherlands and Germany, force the Christian citizens to confront the practice of a rival faith. They also
prompt a keener awareness among the secular citizens of
the phenomenon of the public presence of religion.

(c)   The immigration of 'guest-workers' and refugees,
especially from countries with traditional cultural backgrounds, is the third stimulus for a change of consciousness
among populations. Since the sixteenth century, Europe
had to contend with *confessional* schisms within its own

64

culture and society. As a result of immigration, more strident dissonances between different *religions* are combined
with the challenge of a *pluralism of ways of life* which is
typical of immigrant societies. This goes beyond the challenge of a *pluralism of religious confessions*. In European
societies, which have not yet completed the painful transition to post-colonial immigrant societies, the issue of the
tolerant coexistence of different religious communities is
exacerbated by the difficult problem of integrating immigrant cultures into the host society. While coping with the
pressures of globalized labor markets, social integration
has to be accomplished also under the humiliating conditions of growing social inequality. But that is another story.

Until now I have adopted the perspective of a sociological
observer who tries to answer the question why largely
secularized societies can nevertheless be described as
'post-secular'. In these societies religion retains a certain
public influence and relevance, while the secularistic certainty that religion will disappear everywhere in the world
as modernization accelerates is losing ground. A very different, namely a normative, question demands our attention from the perspective of *participants*: How *should* we
understand ourselves as members of a post-secular society,
and what *must* we expect from one another if we want to
ensure that social relations in firmly entrenched nation–
states remain civil in spite of the growth of cultural and
religious pluralism?

All European societies are confronted with this question today. While writing this essay, I read three different
news items over a single weekend. President Sarkozy is
dispatching 4,000 additional policemen to the notorious
Parisian *banlieues* plagued by rioting Algerian youths; the
Archbishop of Canterbury is recommending that the
British parliament adopt parts of Sharia family law for its
local Muslim population; and a fire broke out in a tene-
ment block in Ludwigshafen in which nine Turks, four of
them children, met their deaths, prompting deep

suspicion and outrage, not to mention genuine dismay, among the Turkish media despite the fact that the cause of the fire remains unclear; this led the Turkish prime minster to make a visit to Germany, and his ambivalent campaign speech in a stadium in Cologne itself triggered a strident response in the German press.

These debates have assumed a sharper tone since the terrorist attacks of 9/11. In the Netherlands, the murder of Theo van Gogh on 2 November 2004 kindled a passionate public discussion, not only concerning the victim but also concerning Mohammed Bouyeri, the assassin, and Ayaan Hirsi Ali, the actual target of the hatred. That debate assumed a character of its own,[12] and its ripples spread beyond the country's borders and unleashed a European-wide debate.[13] What interests me is the assumptions informing this discussion on 'Islam in Europe' which render it so explosive. But before I can address the philosophical core of the mutual recriminations, I must first outline more clearly the shared starting point of the parties to the conflict – namely their commitment to the separation between church and state.

3 From an Uneasy modus *vivendi* to a Balance between Shared Citizenship and Cultural Difference

The secularization of state power was the appropriate response to the confessional wars of the early modern period. The principle of the 'separation between church and state' was realized gradually and assumed a different form in each national legal system. To the extent that the government assumed a secular character, the religious minorities, which were at first merely tolerated, progressively acquired more rights – first the freedom to practice their own religion in private, then the right of religious expression, and finally equal rights to exercise their religion in public. A historical review of this protracted process, which lasted into the twentieth century, can teach us something about the *preconditions* for this valuable achievement of extending inclusive religious freedom to all citizens alike.

Immediately following the Reformation, the state confronted the basic task of pacifying a society split along confessional lines – in other words, of securing law and order. In the context of the current debate, the Dutch writer Margriet de Moor reminded her fellow citizens of these beginnings:

> Tolerance is often mentioned in the same breath as respect, yet our version of tolerance, which has its roots in the sixteenth and seventeenth centuries, is not based on respect. On the contrary, we used to hold a deep hatred of other people's religion. Catholics and Calvinists did not have an ounce of respect for the views of the other side, and our eighty years war was not just an uprising against Spain but a bloody Jihad of Orthodox Calvinists against Catholicism.[14]

It remains to be seen what Margriet de Moor means here by 'respect'.

As regards law and order, the state authority had to take a neutral stance even where it remained intertwined with the dominant religion in the country. The state had to disarm the quarrelling parties, invent arrangements to ensure amicable social relations between the hostile confessions, and monitor their precarious coexistence. In society, each of the antagonistic subcultures could settle into a niche of its own in such a way that they remained estranged *from one another.* The point I want to stress is that precisely this modus vivendi proved to be inadequate when the constitutional revolutions of the late eighteenth century spawned a new political order, which subjected the fully secularized powers of the state to the rule of law and to the democratic will of the people.

This constitutional state is able to guarantee its citizens equal freedom of religion only under the proviso that they no longer barricade themselves up within the self-enclosed lifeworlds of their religious communities and seal themselves off from each other. All subcultures, whether religious or not, are expected to loosen their hold on their individual members so that the latter can recognize each other *reciprocally as citizens* in civil society, hence as members of *one and the same* political community. In their role as democratic citizens, they give themselves those laws which enable them as private citizens to preserve their identity in the context of their own particular culture and worldview and to respect each other. This new relation between democratic government, civil society, and subcultural self-sufficiency is the key to the correct understanding of the two motives which compete with each other today, even though they are supposed to be complementary. For the universalist project of the political Enlightenment in no way contradicts the particularist sensibilities of multiculturalism, provided that the latter is understood in the correct way.

The *liberal* rule of law already guarantees religious freedom as a basic right, which means that the fate of religious minorities no longer depends on the indulgence of a more or less tolerant state authority. Yet it is the *democratic* state that first makes possible the impartial application of this principle.[15] In particular cases – for example, when Turkish communities in Berlin, Cologne, or Frankfurt want to move their places of worship out of backyards by building mosques which are visible from afar – the issue is no longer the principle per se, but its fair application. However, plausible reasons for defining what should or should not be tolerated can only be ascertained by means of the deliberative and inclusive procedures of democratic will formation. The principle of tolerance is first freed from the suspicion of being merely an expression of condescension when the conflicting parties meet as equals in the process of reaching an agreement with each other.[16] How the boundary between the positive freedom of religion (that is, the right to exercise one's own faith) and the negative liberty not to be encumbered by the religious practices of members of other faiths should be drawn in concrete cases is always a matter of controversy. But in a democracy those affected, however indirectly, are themselves involved in the decision-making process.

Of course, 'toleration' is not only a question of enacting and applying laws; it must be practiced in everyday life. Toleration means that believers, members of other religions, and non-believers must concede each other's right to observe convictions, practices, and ways of life which they themselves reject. This concession must be supported through a shared basis of mutual recognition which makes it possible to overcome repugnant dissonances. The kind of recognition required must not be confused with *esteem* for an alien culture and way of life, or for rejected convictions and practices.[17] We need to show tolerance only towards worldviews we consider wrong and habits we do not appreciate. The basis of recognition is not esteem for this or that quality or achievement, but an awareness of belonging to an inclusive community of citizens with equal rights in which each is accountable to everybody else for her political utterances and actions.[18]

This is easier said than done. The equal inclusion of *all* citizens in civil society not only calls for a political culture which prevents liberal attitudes from being confused with indifference. Inclusion can be achieved only if certain material conditions are also met: among other things, full integration in kindergartens, schools, and universities in order to offset social disadvantages; and equal access to the labor market. However, in the present context I am primarily concerned with the image of an inclusive civil society in which equal citizenship and cultural difference complement each other in the correct way.

As long as a substantial proportion of the German citizens of Turkish origin and Muslim faith take their political orientation more from their old home country than from their new one, for example, the corrective votes required to expand the range of values of the dominant political culture will be lacking in the public sphere and at the ballot box. Without the inclusion of minorities in civil society, two complementary processes will not be able to develop hand in hand – namely the opening of the political community to a difference-sensitive inclusion of foreign minority cultures on the one hand, and the liberalization of these subcultures to a point where they encourage their individual members to exercise their equal rights to participate in the political life of the larger community on the other.

4 Philosophical Background Assumptions of the *Kulturkampf* between Radical Multiculturalism and Militant Secularism

In answering the question of how we should understand ourselves as members of a post-secular society we can take our cue from these two *interlocking* processes. The ideological parties which confront each other in public debates today, however, pay scarcely any attention to how the two processes intermesh. The multiculturalist party appeals to the protection of collective identities and accuses the other side of 'Enlightenment fundamentalism'; the secularists, by contrast, insist on the uncompromising inclusion of minorities in the existing political culture and accuse their opponents of a 'multiculturalist betrayal' of the core values of the Enlightenment.

Multiculturalists fight for an even-handed adjustment of the legal system to the claim of cultural minorities to equal treatment. They warn against a policy of enforced assimilation with uprooting consequences. The secular state, they claim, must not promote the integration of minorities into the egalitarian community of citizens so vigorously that it tears individuals out of the contexts in which they form their identities. From this communitarian perspective, a policy of abstract integration is open to the charge that it subjects minorities to the imperatives

of the majority culture. Today, however, the multiculturalists are on the defensive: 'Not only academics, but politicians and newspaper columnists likewise consider the
Enlightenment a fortress to be defended against Islamic
extremism.'[19] This reaction, in turn, brings the critique of
'Enlightenment fundamentalism' into play. For example,
Timothy Garton Ash argues in the *New York Review of
Books* that 'even Muslim women contradict the way in
which Hirsi Ali attributes her oppression to Islam instead
of the respective national, regional or tribal culture'.[20] In
fact Muslim immigrants cannot be integrated into a
western society in defiance of their religion, but only
together with it.

On the other hand, the secularists fight for a color-blind
political inclusion of all citizens, irrespective of their
cultural origin and religious membership. This side warns
against the consequences of a 'politics of identity' which
goes too far in adapting the legal system to the preserva-
tion of the intrinsic characteristics of minority cultures.
From this 'laicistic' point of view, religion must remain
exclusively a private matter. Thus Pascal Bruckner rejects
cultural rights because these supposedly give rise to parallel societies – to 'small, self-isolated social groups, each of
which adheres to a different norm'.[21] Bruckner roundly
condemns multiculturalism as an 'anti-racist racism',
though his attack applies at most to those extremist multiculturalists who advocate the introduction of collective
cultural rights. Such a form of species protection for
entire cultural groups would in fact curtail the right of
their individual members to choose a way of life of their
own.[22]

Thus both of the conflicting parties pretend to fight for
the same goal, a liberal society which allows autonomous
citizens to coexist in a civilized manner. Yet they are
locked in a *Kulturkampf* which resurfaces with every new
political controversy. They argue bitterly over whether
preserving cultural identity should have priority over
enforcing shared citizenship or vice versa, although it is

clear that these two aspects are interlinked. The discussion acquires its polemical edge from contradictory philosophical premises which the opponents rightly or wrongly attribute to one another. Ian Buruma has made the interesting observation that, following 9/11, an academic debate on the Enlightenment, on modernity and post-modernity, migrated from the university to the market-place.[23] The debate was stoked by problematic background assumptions: a cultural relativism pepped up with a critique of reason on the one side, and a secularism ossified into a critique of religion on the other.

The radical reading of multiculturalism often relies on the mistaken notion of the 'incommensurability' of world-views, discourses, or conceptual schemes. From this con-textualist perspective, cultural ways of life appear to be semantically closed universes, each of which holds fast to its own unique standards of rationality and truth claims. Therefore each culture is supposed to exist for itself as a semantically sealed whole, cut off from discursive pro-cesses of reaching an understanding with other cultures. Apart from unstable compromises, submission or conver-sion are supposedly the only alternatives for terminating conflicts between such cultures. Given this premise, radical multiculturalists can see nothing in universalist validity claims such as the arguments for the universality of democracy and human rights – except the imperialist power claim of a dominant culture.

Ironically, this relativistic reading inadvertently robs itself of the standards required by a critique of the unequal treatment of cultural minorities. In our post-colonial immigrant societies, discrimination against minorities is generally rooted in prevailing cultural prejudices which lead to a selective application of the established constitu-tional principles. If the universalist thrust of these prin-ciples is not even taken seriously, then there is no vantage point from which the illegitimate entanglement of the interpretation of the constitution with the prejudices of the majority culture can be uncovered.

There is no need to go into the philosophical reasons for the untenability of a cultural relativism derived from a post-modern critique of reason.[24] However, this position is interesting for the further reason that it explains a peculiar switch of political allegiances. Faced with Islamist terrorism, some of the leftist 'multiculturalists' turned into bellicose liberal hawks, and even entered into an unexpected alliance with the neoconservative 'Enlightenment fundamentalists'. Evidently, in the battle against Islamic fundamentalists these converts were able to embrace the culture of the Enlightenment they had once combated (like the conservatives) as their own 'western culture' because they had always rejected its universalist claims: 'The Enlightenment has become attractive specifically because its values are not just universal, but because they are "our", i.e., European, Western values.'[25]

Needless to say, this critique does not apply to those 'laicistic' intellectuals of French origin for whom the pejorative term 'Enlightenment fundamentalists' was originally coined. However, a certain militancy on the part of these guardians of a universalist Enlightenment tradition is also based on a questionable philosophical background assumption. From their viewpoint, religion must withdraw from the political arena into the private domain because, cognitively speaking, it represents a historically obsolete 'intellectual formation' (a past *Gestalt des Geistes*, in Hegel's terms). Although from the normative standpoint of a liberal constitution religion must be tolerated, it cannot claim to provide a cultural resource for the self-understanding of any truly modern intellectual formation.

5 Complementary Learning Processes: Religious and Secular Mentalities

This philosophical position does not depend on how one judges the empirical observation that religious citizens and communities continue to make relevant contributions to public opinion and to political decision-making even in societies in which secularization is far advanced. Whether or not one regards the predicate 'post-secular' as an appropriate description of western European societies, one can be convinced, for philosophical reasons, that religious communities owe their enduring influence exclusively to the obstinate, but sociologically explicable, survival of pre-modern modes of thought. Either way, the substance of faith is scientifically discredited from the standpoint of secularism. The status of religious traditions as unworthy of serious scientific consideration provokes secularism into a polemical attitude towards religious individuals and traditions which still lay claim to a significant public role.

I make a terminological distinction between 'secular' and 'secularist'. Unlike the neutral stance of a secular or unbelieving person who regards religious validity claims agnostically, secularists adopt a polemical stance towards religious doctrines which retain a certain public influence even though their claims cannot be scientifically justified. Today secularism often appeals to a 'hard', that is, scientifically grounded, version of naturalism. In this case, in contrast to that of cultural relativism, there is no need to comment on the philosophical background.[26] For what interests me in the present context is whether a secularist devaluation of religion, were it one day to be shared by the vast majority of secular citizens, is at all compatible with the post-secular balance between shared citizenship and cultural difference which I have outlined. Or would the secularistic mindset of a relevant portion of the citizenry be just as unappetizing for the normative self-understanding of a post-secular society as the fundamentalist tendencies of a mass of religious citizens? This question taps into deeper roots of the present unease than does any 'multiculturalist drama'.

It is to the credit of the secularists that they, too, vehemently insist on the indispensability of including all

74

citizens as equals in civil society. Because a democratic order cannot simply be *imposed* on its authors, the constitutional state confronts its citizens with the expectations of an ethics of citizenship that reaches beyond mere obedience to the law. Religious citizens and communities must do more than merely conform to the constitutional order in a superficial way. They must appropriate the secular legitimation of constitutional principles under the premises of their own faith.[27] It is a well-known fact that the Catholic church embraced liberalism and democracy only with the Second Vatican Council in 1965. It was no different with the Protestant churches in Germany. Many Muslim communities still have to undergo this painful learning process. Certainly, the realization is also dawning in the Islamic world that today a historical–hermeneutic approach to the teaching of the Qur'an is necessary. However, the discussion concerning a desirable Euro-Islam alerts us once again to the fact that it is the religious communities themselves that will decide whether they can recognize their 'true faith' in a reformed faith.[28]

When we think of such a shift from a traditional to a more reflexive form of religious consciousness, the model of the change in epistemic attitudes within the Christian churches of the West following the Reformation springs to mind. But such a change in mentality cannot be prescribed, nor can it be politically manipulated or forced through by law; at best it is the result of a learning process. Moreover, it appears as a 'learning process' only from the point of view of a secular self-understanding of modernity. With the cognitive preconditions of an ethics of democratic citizenship we run up against the limits of a normative political theory which can justify only rights and duties. Learning processes can be fostered, but they cannot be morally or legally ordered.[29]

However, don't we also have to turn the tables? Is it only religious traditionalism that has to undergo a learning process but not secularism too? Don't the very same normative expectations we have of an inclusive civil society forbid a secularistic devaluation of religion as much as, for example, the religious rejection of the equal status of men and women? At any rate, a *complementary* learning process is required on the secular side – assuming that we do not confuse the neutrality of the secular state towards competing religious worldviews with the banishing of all religious contributions from the political public sphere.

To be sure, the domain of a state which controls the legitimate means of coercion must not be opened up to the strife between different religious communities, for otherwise the government could become the executive arm of a religious majority which imposes its will on the opposition. In a constitutional state, all *enforceable* legal norms must be capable of being formulated and publicly justified in a language intelligible to all of the citizens. Yet the state's neutrality does not speak against the permissibility of religious utterances within the political public sphere, provided that a clear separation remains between the institutionalized consultative and decision-making process at the parliamentary, judicial, ministerial, and administrative levels and the informal flows of political communication and opinion-formation among the broader public of citizens. The 'separation between church and state' calls for a filter between these two spheres which allows only 'translated', hence secular, contributions from among the confused din of voices within the public sphere to find their way onto the formal agendas of the institutions of the state.

Two reasons speak in favor of such a liberal practice. On the one hand, those who are neither willing nor able to separate their moral convictions and vocabulary into profane and religious strands must be permitted to participate in political will formation even if they use religious language. On the other, the democratic state should not over-hastily reduce the polyphonic complexity of the range of public voices, for it cannot be sure whether in doing so it would not cut society off from scarce resources for generating meanings and shaping identities. Especially regarding vulnerable domains of social life, religious traditions have the power to provide convincing articulations of moral sensitivities and solidaristic intuitions. What causes difficulties for secularism, then, is the expectation that the secular citizens in civil society and in the political arena must be able to encounter their religious fellow citizens face to face as equals.

Secular citizens who encountered their fellow citizens with the reservation that the latter cannot be taken seriously as modern contemporaries because of their religious mindset would regress to the level of a mere modus vivendi and abandon the basis of mutual recognition constitutive for shared citizenship. Secular citizens should not exclude *a fortiori* that even religious utterances may have semantic contents and convert personal intuitions capable of being translated and introduced into secular discourse. Thus, if all is to go well, each side must accept an interpretation of the relation between faith and knowledge from its own perspective, which enables them to live together in a self-reflective manner.

6
European Politics at an Impasse: A Plea for a Policy of Graduated Integration*

I am not appearing here this afternoon in the observer role of a social scientific expert who offers advice to the active politician, but as an intellectual who is responsible for the normative insights gleaned from a broader perspective rather than for the pragmatic details of pressing problems. The division of labor between a minister who has to make his decisions on a daily basis and is judged by the success of his policies and a citizen holding forth more or less without consequences whose adult political life coincides with the history of this republic, gives me the freedom to let my thoughts range somewhat more freely in space and time.[1]

First I will first discuss the European deadlock which would not be overcome even by the Lisbon Treaty (I), before I turn to the internal problems (II) and to the external challenges to which the EU must find answers (III). I will round off this picture with three scenarios for a future world order (IV), and from this enlarged perspective I will develop arguments for a policy of graduated integration (V).

*This text formed the basis of my introductory presentation for a conversation with German Foreign Minister Frank-Walter Steinmeier, in which I participated at the invitation of the cultural forum of the SPD at the Willi Brandt House in Berlin, on 23 November 2007.

I Why the Lisbon Treaty Does Not Solve the Real Problems

The Federal Government and its foreign minister are rightly proud of the fact that the groundwork for the Lisbon Treaty was laid during the German presidency of the EU Council of Ministers. Thanks to this fact, there is now the prospect that at least 'the substance' (as it is put) of the failed draft constitution can be converted into ordinary European law. Judged by the predicament in which European politics found itself as a result of the self-castigating reactions of bewildered governments to the outcome of the French and Dutch referenda, setting the reform treaty on the road to ratification is an undoubted diplomatic success. At the same time, there is no room for complacency.

Assuming that it is ratified, the Lisbon Treaty will bring about a welcome institutional reform in 2009 which, as regards the details of voting rights, will be completed by 2017. In this way the governments which sign on to the treaty will have belatedly achieved the goal of an organizational reform which the fifteen-member EU failed to agree upon at the Nice Summit. The twenty-seven-member EU now hopes to regain, at least in domestic policy, the minimum level of executive power which had already been achieved, but which was jeopardized by the enlargement made in order to include twelve new member states. The aim is to promote the willingness of the political elites concerned to compromise and to increase the overall level of efficiency of the EU through suitable organizations and procedures.

What the reform treaty leaves completely unaffected, however, is the mentality and the participation of the populations. For the treaty solves neither of the two problems which, apart from the enhancement of the efficiency of the administrative apparatus, should be solved as a matter of priority by a constitution – not to mention the

79

prospects which those in the 'federalist' camp associate with the potential more than with the wording of the constitutional treaty.[2] It is no accident that the idea of the constitution alone was enough to provoke a pronounced emotional rejection among the Eurosceptics – and not just in Great Britain. The constitution was originally supposed to create the preconditions for: (a) a change in the way politics that has been conducted until now; and (b) a decision concerning the final form (or *finalité*) of the European Union.[3]

(a) Even though the founders of the EU envisaged the ambitious project of a United States of Europe, the process of European unification has in fact taken the sober form of the incremental creation of a common economic zone (with a partly shared currency). The liberal economic forces driving this mutually beneficial dynamics were sufficiently strong to ensure the construction of the requisite institutions 'from above', through an agreement between the political elites of the member states. The political union arose as an elite project above the heads of the peoples concerned, and it continues to operate with the democratic deficits resulting from the essentially intergovernmental and bureaucratic character of the legislative process. The eastwards enlargement, with the attendant crasser disparities in wealth and the increased diversity of interests, gave rise to a growing need for integration which made clear the limits of the willingness to support redistributive policies. Conflicts and tensions arose which could not be dealt with through the established mechanisms.

Thus a political constitution was supposed to create European citizens out of bearers of mauve-coloured passports, and the mobilization of citizens during the constitution-founding process could already have contributed to this goal. The intention, at any rate, was to promote a higher level of participation from citizens across national frontiers in a more visible process of political will formation in Strasbourg and Brussels. Instead of this, the slimmed-down reform treaty now definitively sets the seal on the elitist character of a political process which is remote from the populations. The negotiation procedure, the failure to conduct referenda even where they are actually called for, the bizarre rejection of already established communal symbols (such as the flag and the anthem), finally the national exclusion clauses and the deflationary publicity campaigns employed by some of the governments to sell the result of Lisbon at home – all of this reinforces the established political modus operandi and renders conclusive the fearful decoupling of the European project from the formation of opinion and will by the citizens.

Never before, at turning points in the unification process, has European politics been conducted in such a blatantly elitist and bureaucratic manner as on this occasion. In this way the political class is sending the signal that it is the privilege of the governments to decide the future destiny of Europe behind closed doors. To be sure, the competences of the European Parliament are supposed to be extended; but in the past, too, the citizens did not, and were not able to, register similar enhancements of the powers of the Parliament. For, until the usual spectrum of opinions and relevant issues within the national public spheres is broadened and until the public spheres become responsive to one another, the citizens derive no benefit from a formally strengthened status of the Parliament.

(b)   The second political goal envisaged by the European constitution has also been a failure. The reconfiguration of the elitist project into a mode of politics closer to the citizenry was supposed to create the preconditions for answering the central question concerning the *finalité* of the unification process. The piqued silence of the governments concerning the future of Europe masks the profound conflict over goals which is primarily responsible for the current paralysis of the Union. The 'sovereign

81

subjects of the treaties' are well aware that they are dead-locked over the issues of the final borders of the Union and of what competences should be transferred to the EU in order to facilitate joint policies. The so-called integra-tionists, who have a preference for joint policies and accord priority to the deepening of the Union, and the Euroscep-tics are blocking each other. From a strategic point of view, however, the party in favor of enlargement, which is led by Great Britain, has the advantage that a politics of nondecision works to its advantage.[4] The integrationists are compelled either to take the initiative or to end up as the losers in this undeclared conflict.

Of course, we must be careful not to caricature the positions of the two parties concerned. A federal nation–state like the Federal Republic of Germany cannot provide the model for a Union comprising twenty-seven, and soon twenty-eight and more developed nation–states which are acutely aware of their language and history. The aim of the integrationists is not a federal state but institutions and procedures which build on democratic foundations and make possible a joint foreign and security policy, a gradual harmonization of taxation and economic policy, and a corresponding alignment of the social welfare systems. According to the integrationist program, an enhancement of the regulatory powers of the EU is sup-posed to subject the increased mobility of the factors of production and the joint currency, which is at present under the control of the European Central Bank, to a political framework which already exists in other eco-nomic regions of similar size. In external relations, a foreign and security policy subject to majority decisions is supposed to reduce the current imbalance between the economic and the global political weight of the Union. On the other hand, even the Eurosceptics realize that the EU, in its current form, has outgrown a mere economic com-munity a long time ago. They justify their preference for continuing the dynamics of enlargement by appealing to successes in civilizing politics and to the increase in prosperity in the countries which have been the beneficiaries of the southwards and eastwards enlargements, and which now serve as models to be emulated by their neighbors.

However, the smoldering conflict over the future of Europe gains additional explosiveness from more deep-seated conflicts of interests rooted, if not already in size and geographical location, then in the divergent developmental paths of the nation–states and in diverse national historical memories. This is in no need of further explanation in the case of Great Britain's manifest preference for a policy of global free trade conducted in close cooperation with the United States. Poland, on the other hand, is an example of the characteristic tendency of the accession countries to guard their recently acquired national sovereignty jealously.[5] These historically explicable differences are perfectly understandable and are, of course, no grounds for criticism. But the two camps within the EU must ask themselves how they want to deal with their disagreement.

II Objections

Those who advocate a politics of 'more of the same' take issue both with the analysis and with the conclusion that the two most urgent problems which should have been solved by a political constitution will continue to plague us even after the adoption of the reform treaty. They maintain instead that the alleged democratic deficit is merely an artefact of false normative standards and that an uninterrupted dynamics of enlargement must be seen in the light of the goals of the pacification and development in eastern Europe, in the Middle East, and ultimately in the whole Mediterranean region.

The first objection stands or falls with the plausibility of the distinction between 'technical' issues free from strong legitimation requirements on the one hand, and the genuine 'political' questions which affect people directly

83

and hence must be decided democratically – on the other. Because the European Commission, the European Court of Justice, and the European Central Bank – so it is argued – are primarily concerned with technical issues of institutionalizing and monitoring competitiveness and with ensuring currency stability, we can confidently leave this job to the experts. As long as the EU institutions function smoothly as a whole, this output legitimation, coupled with the role of the democratically legitimate member states, satisfies all demands that could be made on the basis of democratic principles. The citizens are, in any case, more interested in policies relating to taxation, jobs, retirement benefits, and health care. But, since these remain within the competence of the member states which can ensure output legitimation, there is no gap between the indirect legitimation of the members of the council and the direct, but weak, legitimation of the parliament, which is at least selectively involved in the legislative process.[6]

This argument overlooks the fact that the division of competences between the European and the national levels itself reflects an essentially political decision. The fact that the decision is withdrawn from the control of the actors concerned gives rise to an appearance of tasks calling for 'technical' solutions. But the supposedly technical decisions at the European level are decidedly political in nature. For they limit the ability of the nation–states and of their citizens to regulate the conditions under which external costs of free market exchanges are generated which are then shuffled off onto the national level. Thus the nation–states could regain their lost regulatory competences as members of a European Union only if they agreed to harmonize their taxation and economic policies, to align their social policies, and to set certain controls on the European Central Bank.

The second argument also loses its appeal on closer examination. Viewed in retrospect, it is true that the enlargement of the EU towards the South (to include

84

Greece, Spain, and Portugal) and later towards the East proved to be in the mutual interest of core and periphery. All things considered, it had the effect of exporting stability, freedom, and growing prosperity to the new member states, and it opened up new markets for the old. According to this logic, the enlargement process was, as it were, self-perpetuating. With each new enlargement, the disparities between the enlarged core and the new periphery again prompt the desire to develop the region beyond the extended EU frontiers into a stability and buffer zone (as is shown, among other things, by Poland's interest in the accession of Ukraine and by Slovenia's interest in the EU's willingness to entertain the accession of Serbia).[7]

But the objection downplays the fact that, until now, this dynamics of development involved complementary steps of enlargement and consolidation. With every increase in divergence, with the increasing diversity of social and economic interests, of national languages and cultures, and of historically shaped identities, the risk of aggravated conflicts also increases. This is why, in the past, the progressive enlargement of the EU always prompted moves towards a deeper integration. But the further the integration progresses and the more the core becomes dependent on the periphery, the less harmoniously do the countervailing trends of enlargement and consolidation complement each other. The costs of integration increase disproportionately to enlargement:

> The contradiction between enlargement and deeper integration, which could be overcome only through markedly higher financial expenditures, leads to a trilemma for the EU. The latter faces the choice between engaging in more redistribution ... or contenting itself with a modest level of integration, or abandoning the idea of uniform integration in favor of graduated integration.[8]

Thus it remains the case that both of the problems to which the reform treaty fails to provide a solution – the democratic deficit and the unresolved issue of *finalité* – have to be taken seriously. Since the reform treaty tends to cement the existing gap between political elites and citizens and does not pave the way for a political decision concerning the future shape of Europe, the unresolved problems will either lead surreptitiously to a devolution of the level of integration already achieved or heighten the awareness of a painful alternative. The European governments

• will either stick to their policy of nondecision and in the process fall back ever more blatantly into the familiar pattern of national power politics,
• or their stalemate will force them to summon the citizens themselves to a vote.

Before I discuss the global political arguments which, likewise, speak for continuing the process of European unification, I would like to mention in passing a third objection which, if it were correct, would render the alternative of a deeper integration moot. From a conservative nationalist point of view, the European Union can continue to exist only as a hybrid construction founded in essence on international treaties, because the diversity of historically evolved nations prevents it from developing an identity of its own.[9]

Not even incessant repetition renders this stubborn objection more plausible. In Germany, the objection takes the form of the assertion that a 'European people' does not exist. This is symptomatic of the tenaciousness of the Romantic background philosophy of the German historical school.[10] Ironically enough, the idea of the spirit of the people [*Volksgeist*] was itself an important component of nineteenth-century historiography, which placed itself at the service of the construction of new collective identities by producing proud national histories. The derivative appearance of naturalness of a national consciousness developed by historians and disseminated through the

86

modern mass media disguises the artificial character of this form of consciousness. The newly-constituted collective identity did in fact, for the first time, lend concrete form, emotion, and conviction to the abstract legal concept of civic solidarity. Thus there is no reason to assume that the emergence of a sense of political solidarity must come to a halt at the frontiers of the nation–state. Why shouldn't the empty shell of the European citizenship, which has been established for some time, become filled in a similar way with the awareness that all European citizens now share the same political fate?[11]

However, the development of a European-wide political public sphere – that is, of a communicative network extending across national boundaries and specializing in the relevant questions – is of central importance for the emergence of such a European identity, however weak it may be, relatively speaking.[12] It is not enough that common policies are institutionalized in Brussels and Strasbourg and that the European citizens could influence these policies through the election of a parliament with its own factions. If the citizens are to be able to make factual use of their right to vote, and in the process develop a sense of solidarity through this practice, the European decision-making processes must become visible and accessible within the existing national public spheres. A European public sphere can arise only if the national public spheres become responsive *to one another*, which would also remove the obstacle of multilingualism. In this sense, Bernhard Peters differentiates three steps in the communicative promotion of participation:

- governance can take place under public scrutiny only if the national mass media promote awareness of the corresponding policies and alternative decisions through continuous reporting and commentary;
- the citizens will gain access to this politics in their role as European citizens only if the media also provide

them with information concerning the inputs and debates in the other national public arenas;

- a process of deliberative decision-making can develop within a European-wide communicative context only if a discursive exchange of arguments and opinions across national boundaries becomes possible in communication between the respective public arenas.[13]

Finally, this third stage in the convergence of the civil societies will foster an awareness of European commonality, provided that important questions of foreign, social, and tax policy are decided at this level. This calls for new actors, namely interest groups and parties organized at the European level, and other influential organizations, activists, and intellectuals with a pan-European profile. Here too, it is sufficient that the national public spheres should open themselves osmotically to one another. The hierarchical notion of an overarching European public sphere with its own, predominantly English-speaking, media overlaying the national public spheres is misleading. This is why Peters speaks of a 'transnationalization of public spheres'. Although the results of the empirical study he conducted using this analytic apparatus[14] are chastening, they reveal trends which point in the right direction and open up the prospect of the development of a European identity

III The External Challenges

It is not only the problems rendered more acute by the internal dynamics of the unification process that force us to adopt a constructive stance on the dilemma of the unresolved conflict over goals. The global challenges facing Europe also call for a choice between the alternative of passively accepting a creeping devolution and the decision to continue the process of integration. This is why we must confront the question of whether Europe should aspire to more than its current modest role on the global political stage.

The declared unilateralism of the United States – since the announcement of the Bush Doctrine in the Fall of 2002 and the deliberate marginalization of the United Nations; since the invasion of Iraq in violation of international law, the continued violation of humanitarian international law, and a blatant policy of double standards (for example the recognition of India as a nuclear power) – has destroyed the credibility of the normative foundations of western policy. As a catalyst of a new world order, this policy has triggered a social Darwinist lowering of inhibitions towards the use of violence and the reckless pursuit of national interests on all sides. As a result, other continents are increasingly looking expectantly – though thus far in vain – to the new face of the old Europe, which remained unpacified until the middle of the twentieth century.

During the outbreak of the most recent conflict between Israel and Lebanon in July 2006, the governments of Germany, France, Italy, and Spain outdid themselves in their attempts to enhance their image instead of uniting behind the efforts of their own EU foreign policy chief in an attempt to provide a timely counterweight to the delaying tactics of the United States supported by Great Britain. Given the opportunity presented by the fact that, for the first time since the foundation of the state of Israel, a neutral force is stationed in the disputed region and strengthens the negotiating power of third parties, Europe failed once again. The so-called Quartet, which developed a roadmap without consequences for Israel, still offers a comparatively propitious framework. For Europe is represented on it by the EU as a whole, alongside the UN, the USA, and Russia. In the meantime, the governments of Merkel, Sarkozy, and Brown seem to have reverted to old-style nationalist policies, a fact underlined by their competing attempts to court Washington.

The decision of the German red–green coalition government during the (failed) UN reform process under

Kofi Annan to apply – alongside India, Brazil, and Japan – for a permanent seat in the Security Council as the third European member already signaled a shift in the direction of European policy during Joschka Fischer's term as German foreign minister. Clearly the German government had already abandoned any hope of a joint European foreign and security policy. This suggests that the expectations now associated with the institutional upgrading of the office of the EU High Representative for the Common Foreign and Security Policy are even less ambitious. Since this policy is contingent upon unanimous decisions by all of the twenty-seven member states, not even the voice of a vice-president will lend the foreign policy representative any additional weight on the global political stage. This is made abundantly clear by the decision not to confer the title of 'EU Foreign Minister'.[15]

There are two obvious arguments why this important global economic region should also make itself heard politically. (a) First, the nation–states have now almost no chance of ever influencing global political developments on their own; their only remaining hope of promoting their own interests is by pursuing them jointly. (b) Second, the desirable transnational institutionalization of a global domestic policy has no chance in a divided, multicultural, yet differentiated world society unless the small and medium-sized nation–states unite to form regional regimes like the EU, which are capable of acting and negotiating on the global stage.

(a) The confusing, extensive, and increasingly dense network of international organizations which responds to the growing need for coordination in an ever more complex world society has been studied and analyzed in the relevant scholarly literature over the last decade and a half. The authors are more or less in agreement that the larger nation–states remain the most important actors on the global stage. Even compared to the most economically influential multinational corporations, states enjoy the advantage being of monopolists of political power who control legitimate means of regulation and sanction. When it comes to collectively-binding conflict resolution and dealing constructively with matters in need of regulation, there are no functional equivalents for the competences based on the possession of 'law' and 'political power'. On the other hand, states have lost much of their autonomous decision-making power in the transition from the national to the postnational constellation.[16]

The sovereignty of the subjects of international law was restricted not just in a formal sense within the context of the international community – for example, as regards the elementary right to conduct war and make peace. Nation–states have in fact lost a considerable portion of their controlling and steering capabilities in the functional domains in which they were able to make more or less independent decisions until the most recent major phase of globalization (during the final quarter of the twentieth century). This holds for all of the classical functions of the state, from safeguarding peace and physical security to guaranteeing freedom, the rule of law, and democratic legitimation. Since the demise of embedded capitalism and the associated shift in the relation between politics and the economy in favor of globalized markets, the state has also been affected, perhaps most deeply of all, in its role as an interventionary state, which must ensure the social security of its citizens already for reasons of legitimation.[17]

Physical security within the respective national territories can no longer be assured without international cooperation in combatting the cross-border risks of large-scale technology, the global spread of epidemics, worldwide organized crime, and the new decentralized terrorist networks; moreover, the porous borders are becoming less capable of withstanding the pressure of the massive streams of migration. The national legal systems have been for a long time overlaid by the stipulations of international law and infiltrated by international legal precedents. The national procedures of democratic will formation and control are much too weak to meet the need for legitimation generated by the local impacts of international regulations. The deregulation of the markets, especially of the global financial markets, limits the scope for intervention from national governments and loosens their grip on the tax revenues of their most successful enterprises.

Faced with these new dependencies, the nation–states can try to adapt as smoothly as possible to the postnational constellation by using the means already at their disposal. Thus Germany is fighting a losing battle to keep up with the social and political costs of economic globalization. A more effective strategy for nation–states is to offset their lost functions by merging into the existing international networks as global co-players. In this way they would exploit the political opportunities which have developed at the supranational level to fill the vacuum created by the rapidly developing markets and by the need for a regulation of global networks.

Two characteristic forms of 'governance in transnational spaces' have developed. Either each nation–state sends representatives to multilateral organizations in order to pursue its aims by forming coalitions – this is where the terminology of the G8, the G22, and the G77 comes in – and by exercising strategic influence on agenda setting and on the conduct of negotiations; or they unite with neighbors to form regional alliances in order to pool and mobilize their resources on a permanent basis. Compared with similar cases (for instance the Association of Southeast Asian Nations and the African Union), the European Union is the best example of such a collective form of supranational governance, and thus it serves as a model for similar aspirations in Latin America, Asia, and Africa.

(b)   In this context it is important to observe that global problems are forcing themselves upon us which are difficult to resolve without this second form of supranational governance. Above all, five problems are especially pressing:

- international security;
- global measures to prevent the tipping of vital ecological balances (climate change, drinking water supply, and the like);
- the distribution of scarce energy resources;
- the global implementation of basic human rights; and
- a fair global economic system, which goes beyond ad hoc aid for catastrophes in poverty-stricken regions to address the extreme disparities in wealth and global inequalities in life chances (see the United Nations Millennium Development Goals).

The sheer scope of these problems invites the question of the appropriate institutional framework within which they could be addressed. In my estimation, climate change is the only case in which there is any prospect of a resolution on the basis of an agreement between nation–states, in other words via classical international agreements. The reason for this lies in the physical nature of the problem, which at least limits the room for conflicting interpretations, and in the unavoidability and inclusiveness of the impacts of climate change. None of the parties involved can outrun these consequences, regardless of whether they are natural superpowers, nation–states, or regional regimes. By contrast, I cannot imagine how the other problems could be solved without a thoroughgoing reform of the United Nations and without the establishment of an institutionalized global domestic policy.

   The absurd discrepancy between the pompous rituals of G8 summits and the almost effusive, grotesquely exaggerated expectations associated with these empty, symbolic political events in the media and in the protest milieu is a sure sign of a broad awareness of what is missing. What is lacking is a transnational negotiating body whose composition is sufficiently representative for it to negotiate fair compromises to deal with global problems and for it to implement them in the regions affected. The composition of the most important multilateral organizations, such as the WTO, the World Bank, and the IMF on the one side, and the Security Council on the other, is selective and reflects the asymmetry of existing power relations. Moreover, these are among the numerous specialized organizations whose domains of operation overlap in untransparent ways. At the same time they are already far too specialized, with the result that none of them, in conducting global policy in one field, could keep track of the interferences with decisions in other policy fields, or even address the problem of a harmonization between them. Only once this gap had been filled could we begin to speak of 'governance' beyond the nation–state.

To be sure, individual nation–states can pursue their own interests by adapting more or less successfully to the incremental spread of the mesh of international organizations and networks. But the negotiating power of individual states and their ability to wield threats are insufficient when it comes to constructing an innovative international order designed to respond to the global problems mentioned. Of course, the political weight of an EU empowered to act and negotiate in the domain of foreign policy is required not only for the arduous task of *constructing* a new world order; such a union is even more a functional requirement for the successful operation of a politically constituted world society which could serve as the endpoint of such a process. This brings us to the far-reaching discussion that Kant initiated with his theses concerning a 'cosmopolitan condition'.[18] These and similar reflections on a political constitution for the multinational and multicultural world society immediately invite Hegel's objection concerning the 'impotence of the "ought"'. They have to prove themselves in opposition to other, seemingly more realistic conceptions of a future world order.

94

IV Scenarios of a Future World Order

The expert discussion in jurisprudence long ago absorbed the impulses of philosophy and refined them into the idea of a 'constitutionalization of international law'. I cannot address this topic here.[19] In what follows I would like to confine myself to rebutting the charge of 'idealism'. Starting from the risks of the current global situation, I will compare the political answers of neoconservatism and of so-called realism with the general conception of a politically constituted world society without a world government.

A multicultural world society in which from now on there will be only more-or-less modern societies is emerging before our eyes. Other civilizations are responding to the western pressure to modernize their societies as challenges to which they seek answers by drawing upon their own cultural resources. For *the same* dialectical tension between tradition and modernity from which the occidental form of modernity first emerged is now also operating in other civilizational complexes. This is especially apparent among the East Asian cultures. 'Modernity' is no longer the exclusive possession of the West. Today it constitutes something like an arena in which different civilizations, with their culturally specific adaptations of a common social infrastructure, encounter each other.[20] This leads to cultural tensions between the Jewish–Christian and the Islamic world, for example, or between the cultures of the West and those of the Far East. But Islamic terrorism, and in general the release of the political potential for violence of the major world religions, disguise the fact that the religious coding of cultural tensions is often a reflection of deeper-lying conflicts of interests. The unstable current situation is characterized, above all,

• by the asymmetrical division of power between the pole comprising the superpower and its allies

(Europe, Japan) on the one side, and the poles of the major or emerging powers such as Russia, India, China, and Brazil;

- by the 'external costs' of a capitalist world economy to which there is no longer any alternative, where these costs are organized, in accordance with neoliberal economic ideas, largely in the interests of the developed societies;
- by a global scarcity of energy reserves, coupled with an acceleration in economic development and a rise in global energy usage; and
- by a decentralized proliferation of weapons of mass destruction and an increase in the number of nuclear powers, coupled with a weakening of the controls of the International Atomic Energy Agency.

To each of these destabilizing elements there corresponds a risk, which neoconservatism wishes to counter with a politics of the 'good hegemon'. This kind of risk management shaped the policy of the Bush administration and found expression in a politics marked by a preference for unilateral over multilateral decision-making strategies, military over diplomatic means of conflict resolution, and short-term over long-term calculations of interests. The normative viewpoints offered as pretexts for a justification, such as exporting democracy and implementing human rights, have in the meantime degenerated into sheer ideology. To be sure, the policy of the Bush administration is already shifting towards a 'realist' power politics.

The specter of 'Islamofascism' conjured up by the American neoconservatives continues to function as a surrogate for the communist enemy. However, the strategic maneuvering against Russia (with the missile shield) and the attempts to forge an Israeli–Southern Arab front against Iran and Syria in the Middle East and to play Japan and India off against China in the Far East already reveal the contours of a future US foreign policy largely free from normative rhetoric, but no less nationally oriented and power-conscious.

The 'realist' school of international relations, which was influential in Washington during the Cold War and will regain its influence after Bush, differs from neoconservatism not so much in its goal of consolidating hegemonic power as in its rational choice of means. Moreover, this school pursues the goals of defusing conflicts and promoting stability (even if, like Kissinger in the past, it is willing to countenance considerable normative damage in order to achieve them). During the Cold War, the end state to which realism aspired, notwithstanding its instability, condensed into the image of the nuclear balance between the competing social systems. But the weakness of the realist approach becomes apparent as soon as we pose the question of what the equilibrium condition to which such a policy is supposed to aspire would look like today, in a multicultural world society. The current global situation cuts the ground out from under a conception which was tailored to the circumstances of the Cold War.

The dream of hegemonic liberalism in a world pacified under American leadership has had a rude awakening in Iraq. Every conception of a unipolar world order is invalidated by the complexity of world society. The basic assumptions of 'realism' state that justice between nations is impossible in principle and the only possible balance is achievable exclusively through a militarily policed equilibrium of interests based on power politics. On these assumptions, Carl Schmitt's theory of hemispheres still seems to offer the best approximation to the scenario of a desirable global order – though only at a first glance, because the basic assumptions of realism bypass contemporary reality.[21]

Schmitt no longer conceived of the 'hemispheres' as state territories but as 'spheres of influence' under the domination of imperial powers and their 'strong ideas'. In each case, a natural central power set apart by its historical achievements is supposed to assert its preeminence over the periphery of dependent nations and populations, according to the standards of its own, incommensurable conception of justice. On this approach, these modern heirs of the ancient empires would defend their hemi-spheres, cultures, and forms of life in a sovereign manner, and if necessary with military force, against each other. However, this unstable equilibrium is supposed to be stabilized by a system of hemispheres which transfers the principle of nonintervention from the world of states of classical international law to the international legal sub-jects of the new type.

Quite apart from the fact that this vision of a power-based balance between continental hemispheres disre-gards the threat of asymmetrical warfare,[22] it remains captive to the obsolete notion of the relative independence of the subjects of international law. The supposed realism of such conceptions of equilibrium evaporates in the face of the global problems resulting from the high level of interdependence in a world society which is undergoing differentiation without regard to borders. These problems call for something other than the restraint which an unstable and explosive equilibrium would demand from competing world powers. They call, namely, for coopera-tion within a stable institutional framework. For all global regions and all societies are affected by the impacts of climate change, of the competition for access to scarce energy resources, of wars and civil wars, of failing states, of genocide and crimes against humanity, of the cata-strophic conditions prevalent in the impoverished regions, and of the unwelcome risks and side effects of a produc-tive global economic system. These problems can be solved only through a joint effort on the part of the inter-national community. Even the deeply offended sense of distributive justice – the purely moral weight of the glaring social and economic disparities in a highly stratified world society – will become a difficult burden for the affluent societies to bear in so far as it heightens awareness of the systemic connection between capitalist wealth production and growing disparities, and thus poverty and misery, in those societies as well.

A comparison between the three conceptions leads unavoidably to the conclusion that 'realism' does not have any more convincing an answer to the imperative to cooperate in mastering global challenges than neoconservatism does. Only the revival of the political program which led to the foundation of the United Nations at the initiative of an American president promises to provide an answer.[23] The experiences of the past six decades have made the deficiencies of the existing institutions abundantly clear. There is widespread agreement on the need for reform, if not concerning the details of the long overdue reforms. The world organization must be rendered capable of performing the tasks of international peacekeeping and of implementing basic human rights on a global scale more effectively and less selectively than before. As important as it is controversial is the more far-reaching proposal that the United Nations should be relieved of tasks which it cannot perform – because, by their very nature, they call for a world domestic policy. Among these tasks I count the issues of global energy policy and environmental, financial, and economic policy relevant for distribution.[24]

In these respects there is a need for regulation and positive integration for which at present both the institutional framework and the suitable actors are lacking. The existing political networks are one-sided and specialized, and they form – as in the case of the WTO and the World Bank – multilateral organizations in which the delegates of the most powerful countries have the final say. We lack a representative transnational negotiation system equipped with competences of a sufficiently general kind to enable it to keep track of the overall picture. Only large-scale regional regimes which are both representative and capable of implementing decisions and policies could make such an institution workable. The nation–states must unite at the transnational level to form a manageable number of such global players within the framework of the supranational world organization, hence as members of the international community. Thus, in addition to the natural major powers, we need regimes along the lines of an EU with its own foreign policy.

Of course, this, at present improbable, scenario has a chance of being realised only if the superpower takes a leading role in this reform movement – not simply because it is a superpower capable of carrying others along with it, but because the United States is, historically speaking, an improbable superpower. It is the oldest democracy in the world; it is sustained by idealistic traditions; and it has embraced the spirit of eighteenth-century universalism more than any other nation. Even though the policy of the current administration has flagrantly betrayed this spirit, Bush's addresses to the nation still reflect, in a perverted form, the core of a genuinely American self-understanding, a normative core which was instrumentalized for irresponsible purpose at a moment when an understandably shocked nation was in the grip of neurosis. In any case, a US government aware of the transitoriness of its superpower status cannot ignore the potential considerations which speak for such an agenda. An American government reflecting upon the changed world of the year 2030 cannot wish that China should then conduct itself as Bush's America is doing today. It is, instead, in its own interest to try today to bind the major powers of tomorrow into an international order which no longer needs a superpower.

A serious realistic assessment of the situation, however, also raises the question of whether the USA would undertake such a course without the friendly insistence of a loyal but self-confident ally (a role which could be assumed only by an independent EU equipped with a foreign policy of its own). This suggests that we should overcome the existing mental split in the West in favor of a 'bipolar' commonality, of a West which is determined not to squander its damaged normative credibility any further. Such a bipolar commonality of the West demands that Europe should adopt an unbiased, self-confident view of the United States, a view which is at the same time suffi- ciently self-critical to resist even the slightest temptation of anti-Americanism.

V A Policy of Graduated Integration

No matter how convincing the reasons for a further expansion of the political union may be, they do not offer any operative pointer as to how European policy could find its way out of its current dilemma. The first task is to make a correct diagnosis of the causes of the malaise.

Because the unification process has until now been promoted by political elites, the two unsuccessful refer- enda have reinforced the view that the European consti- tutional project failed because of popular opposition. The draft constitution was correctly criticized for enshrining the basic features of an economic constitution, features which have no place in such a document;[25] however, the two referenda were so much overshadowed by extraneous domestic political controversies and emotions that they could not provide an undistorted expression of opinions concerning Europe. The ratification process did not even advance as far as the critical test case of Great Britain.

The Europe-wide polls conducted since 1992, by con- trast, tell a completely different story. Over this period, the Eurobarometer not only exhibits stable levels of approval among the citizens for the EU membership of their respective countries but also shows that clear majori- ties support a joint European foreign and security policy. This picture has not changed substantially since the east- wards enlargement. Corresponding to it is the support for the constitutional process: in early 2007, 66 percent of those questioned still supported a European constitution (which even represents an increase of 5 percent over the previous year). Analysing these average figures country by country, we find relatively low levels of approval in Great Britain, in the two Scandinavian countries, and perhaps also in Denmark.

Admittedly, questionnaires are of limited value. Polled opinions are particularly unstable when those questioned have little familiarity with the corresponding issues, and thus have given them little thought. The latter is predominantly the case, given the low levels of participation of the citizens in the European decision-making processes, which they perceive as distant. Against this background, the results of the first Europe-wide experiment involving 362 out of 3,500 representative citizens chosen from all twenty-seven member states acquire additional interest. This experiment was conducted in the Fall of 2007, in accordance with the 'before and after' design of James Fishkin's studies with small discussion groups.[26] This procedure fosters the formation of opinions through discussion and stimulates the kind of exchange of arguments for and against that grabs the attention of voters in election campaigns. As is usual with such experiments, there was also a dramatic increase in the level of information of the participants. Among other things, it transpired that the desire of the participants for a stronger role of the EU in foreign policy increased from 55 percent to 63 percent over the course of the deliberation process. What's more, on all issues there was a convergence of opinions among the old and the new member states.

These and similar results suggest that a latent, rather Europe-friendly, mood predominates among the citizens in all of the member states, with the exception of Great Britain and the Scandinavian countries. The governments are the stumbling block, not their populations. The governments shy away from a constructive debate over the future of Europe. Apart from the understandable wariness of political parties when they are faced with imponderable risks, the interest in retaining power may also be at work here, for example the fear among members of government – and especially the foreign minister – of sinking into the insignificance of princelings. Thus in the constituted Europe a strong, authoritative council (incorporating the councils of ministers) must acquire a high public profile in order to provide an arena which can serve as a substitute for the provincial theatres of the national actors. The command bridge of the Commission allows room for only a few actors at a time.

If this analysis is not completely mistaken, then there is only one way to overcome the impasse. The governments have to bite the bullet and give their citizens the opportunity to participate in a referendum to be held concurrently in each of the member states, under the same electoral law. The question to be decided would be whether they want a politically constituted Europe with a directly elected president, its own foreign minister, a stronger harmonization of tax policy, and an alignment of their respective social policies. The proposal would be deemed accepted if it succeeded in winning the 'double majority' of the states and of the votes of the citizens. At the same time, the referendum would be binding only on those member states in which a majority of the citizens voted for the reform. In my estimation, when faced with such an admittedly unpalatable alternative, the eastern European accession countries would also be inclined to align themselves with the center. Thus a policy of graduated integration is not aimed against these countries. Even in a Europe of core and periphery, the countries which initially prefer to remain on the sidelines would, of course, have the option of joining the centre at any time.

My optimism that such a referendum would be accepted is based, among other things, on the fact that the same parties which behave cautiously in government, or with an eye to a future participation in government, would have to fight out in the open once the question of the future of Europe was no longer decided in the cabinets but in the marketplaces. Until now all elections to the European Parliament had been decided more or less on the basis of national issues. It is high time for Europe to be no longer governed only *for* the people.

To be sure, the decision to hold a referendum could be pushed through the European Council only in the teeth of resistance. One means of exerting pressure consists in the treaty provisions which foresee the possibility of a 'closer cooperation' in particular fields. However, it would arouse great suspicion if Germany were to take the initiative – together with the three large Latin European member states in the West and South – towards closer cooperation in the field of foreign and security policy. In view of Germany's size and geographical location, and especially in view of its historical baggage, any movement in this direction is problematic because it would awaken the historically understandable suspicion of its neighbors. That said, the Genscher tradition in German foreign policy (with the exception of its fall from grace with the premature recognition of Croatia) has accumulated a certain capital of trust.

***

Why am I presenting these reflections in the Willi Brandt House? The foreign minister may be inclined to dismiss them as speculative finger exercises; but perhaps in his role as deputy chairman of the SPD he should spare them an afterthought.

The SPD has maneuvered itself into a difficult position with consistently low approval ratings because it has remained too much captive to the established national mindset, even though in this regard it could distinguish itself from The Left to its advantage.[27] In spite of its declared commitments to European policy in its new political program, and in spite of its scattered references to the need to subject the international financial markets to tighter regulation, the SPD – like its sister parties in Great Britain and other western European countries – is trying to absorb the risks of economic globalization for

104

the labor market and for the social security systems within the framework of the nation–state. Couldn't this goal be better achieved by harmonizing the corresponding policies within the larger European economic area, or at least within the Eurozone?

There is still another reason for looking beyond the national garden-fence. The SPD was always a program-based party, and it is losing its clientele because it no longer offers them a comprehensive, forward-looking perspective which satisfies the classic need for justice – one which goes beyond the details of retirement age, day care, and health care reform. I don't mean, as someone who enjoys a higher income, to disregard the tough challenges of social policy. In the midst of one of the most dazzlingly affluent societies, growth in child poverty, growing disparities in the distribution of income and property, an increasing low-wage sector with precarious job security, and the growing segment of those who feel superfluous strikes me as scandalous. But this scandal should be seen as part of the problems which can be solved only if we reverse the global trend of the markets to outstrip the organizational options of politics.[28]

Part III
On Reason in the Public Sphere

7
The Constitutionalization of International Law and the Legitimation Problems of a Constitution for World Society*

With the monstrous mass crimes of the twentieth century, states – as the subjects of international law – forfeited the presumption of innocence which underlies the prohibition on intervention and the immunity against criminal prosecution under international law. To be sure, the development of international law since the end of the Second World War was not merely a response to wars of aggression and mass crimes; the innovations have not been confined to the security and human rights regime of the United Nations. Both within and beyond the United Nations, forms of international governance have developed in the fields of energy, environment, finance, and trade policy; of labor relations; of organized crime; of arms trafficking; of combating epidemics, and so on. Continental alliances between states are also developing in tandem with common markets and currencies. The accelerated incremental growth of international organizations can also be understood as a response to the need for regulation resulting from the increasing interdependence of an emerging world society whose functional subsystems extend across national borders. These innovations in

---

*The text reproduces parts of my reply to the essays in Peter Niesen and Benjamin Herborth (eds), *Anarchie der kommunikativen Freiheit* (Frankfurt am Main: Suhrkamp, 2007), pp. 406–59.

international law bring with them a growing need for intercultural communication and interpretation, between civilizations shaped by one or more of the major world religions.

Over the same period, the sovereignty of the subjects of international law was restricted in more than merely formal ways within the context of the international community – for example, regarding the basic right to conduct war and to make peace. Nation–states have in fact lost a considerable amount of their controlling and steering capabilities in the functional domains in which they could make more or less independent decisions until the most recent major phase of globalization (during the final quarter of the twentieth century).[1] This holds for all of the classical functions of the state, from safeguarding peace and physical security to guaranteeing freedom, the rule of law, and democratic legitimation. Since the demise of embedded capitalism and the associated shift in the relation between politics and the economy in favor of globalized markets, the state has also been affected, perhaps most profoundly, in its role as an interventionary state which is supposed to guarantee the social security of its citizens.

We must take these historical developments into account when it comes to theory-building; thus it is counterproductive to cling to the state-centered tradition of modern political thought. It seems more promising to me to take up Kant's idea of the cosmopolitan constitution at the requisite level of abstraction, in an attempt to detach the notion of a constitutionalization of international law[2] from the idea of a world republic, which is rejected for goods reasons.[3]

On the other hand, the very historical developments alluded to above draw our attention to a resulting problem which remains unsolved. As international institutions form an increasingly dense network and nation–states lose some of their competences, a gap is opening up between the new need for legitimation created by governance beyond the nation–state and the familiar institutions and procedures of legitimation which have until now functioned halfway properly only within the nation–state. From the perspective of democratic theory, the empirically well-confirmed diagnosis of the 'simultaneity of the delegitimation of the nation–state and the need for supranational policies to draw upon the legitimation resources of the nation–state', which Ingeborg Maus has repeatedly emphasized,[4] hits a sore point. For example, the institutions of the European Union are based on the legal foundation of international treaties, but they exercise decision-making powers which intrude so deeply into the social relations of the member states that they can no longer be legitimized on this basis alone.[5]

If the advocates of a constitutionalization of international law are not to write off democracy altogether, they must at least develop models for an institutional arrangement which can secure a democratic legitimation for new forms of governance in transnational spaces. Even without the backing of state sovereignty, the sought-for arrangement must *connect up with* the existing, though inadequate, modes of legitimation of the constitutional state, while at the same time *supplementing* them with its own contributions to legitimation. In what follows, I will first draw upon a proposal for a political constitution for world society which I have developed elsewhere and address a specific objection to it (1); in response to this objection, I will distinguish between the legitimate expectations and demands of cosmopolitan and national citizens respectively, and I will show how potential conflicts between them can be institutionally cushioned and processed (2); finally, I will examine how the legitimation requirements of a democratically constituted world society without a world government could be satisfied – provided that nation–states and their populations undergo certain learning processes (3).

111

1 A Global Three-Level System and Nagel's Problem

The decisive conceptual move – and in this I follow authors like Hauke Brunkhorst[6] – consists in differentiating between the three elements of statehood, democratic constitution, and civic solidarity, which are closely linked in the historical form of the constitutional state. Whereas the political constitution and the solidarity-fostering membership in an association of free and equal legal subjects can also reach beyond national borders, the substance of the state – the decision-making and administrative power of a hierarchically organized authority which enjoys a monopoly on violence – depends ultimately on state infrastructure. To simplify matters, I will use some quotations from an earlier work[7] to recall the non-state conception of a legally constituted international community which obligates nation–states to coexist peacefully and authorizes them – that is, confers upon them the 'sovereignty' – to guarantee the basic rights of their citizens within their territories. The international community would be embodied in a world organization overseeing the performance of these functions and, if necessary, taking measures against rule-violations by individual governments. That said, the competences of the world organization would be confined to these fundamental tasks. For this reason the supranational level must be distinguished from the transnational level within the political system of world society:

> In a multi-level global system, the classical function of the state as the guarantor of security, law, and freedom would be transferred to a *supranational* world organization specialized in securing peace and implementing human rights worldwide. However, the world organization would not have to shoulder the immense burden of a global domestic policy designed to overcome the extreme disparities in wealth within the stratified world society, reverse ecologi-

112

cal imbalances, and avert collective threats, on the one hand, while endeavoring to promote an intercultural discourse on, and recognition of, the equal rights of the major world civilizations, on the other. These problems ... call for a different kind of treatment within the context of *transnational* negotiation systems. They cannot be solved directly by bringing power and law to bear against unwilling or incapable nation–states. They impinge upon the intrinsic logic of functional systems that extend across national borders and the inherent meaning of cultures and world religions. Politics must engage with these issues in a spirit of hermeneutic open-mindedness through the prudent balancing of interests and intelligent regulation. (pp. 333–4)

Whereas the world organization would have a hierarchical structure and its members would make binding law, interactions at the transnational level would be heterarchical. Thus the second important conceptual move consists in distinguishing between domain-specific networks which coordinate the decisions of independent collective actors at the level of expert committees on the one hand and a central negotiation system which performs political tasks beyond merely managing interdependencies on the other:

At present we can observe this in the arena of increasingly numerous and interconnected *transnational* networks and organizations designed to cope with the growing demand for coordination of a world society that is becoming more complex. However, regulation in the form of the 'coordination' of governmental and non-governmental actors is only sufficient to address a particular category of cross-border problems. The largely institutionalized procedures of information exchange, consultation, control, and agreement are sufficient for handling 'technical' issues in a broader sense (such as the standardization of measures, the regulation of telecommunications, disaster prevention, containing epidemics, or combating organized crime). Since the devil is always in the detail, these problems also call for a balancing of conflicting interests.

However, they differ from genuinely 'political' issues that impinge on entrenched interests which are deeply rooted in the structures of national societies, such as, for example, questions of global energy, environmental, financial, and economic policy, all of which involve issues of equitable distribution. These problems of a future world domestic politics call for regulation and positive integration, for which at present both the institutional framework and actors are lacking. The existing political networks are functionally differentiated, multilateral, and at times even inclusive international organizations in which government representatives generally bear the responsibility and have the final word, irrespective of who else is granted admission. At any rate, they do not provide an *institutional framework* for legislative competences and corresponding processes of political will-formation. (pp. 323–4)

According to this proposal, the central negotiation system would exercise competences of a general kind; however, it would combine the flexibility of state governments, which are able to maintain an overview, with the non-hierarchical constitution of a multilateral organization of members with equal rights. Only extensive regional regimes which are both representative and capable of implementing decisions and policies could make such an institution workable. Alongside such 'born' major powers as the United States, China, India, and Russia, neighboring nation–states and whole continents (such as Africa) would have to unite on the model of the EU – albeit a future EU, which has been empowered to speak and act with one voice – in order to satisfy this condition. At any rate, the improbable constellation with which the whole construction stands or falls calls for a certain concentration of political power in the hands of a few global players. This concentration would have to be wrested from the centrifugal forces exerted by the functional differentiation of world society. In order to determine whether we have already passed the point of no return,[8] we must keep track of the systemic as well as of the normative developments:

Even if such a framework were to be established, collective actors capable of implementing such decisions would still be lacking. What I have in mind are *regional or continental regimes* equipped with a sufficiently representative mandate to negotiate for whole continents and to wield the necessary powers of implementation for large territories. Politics cannot intentionally meet the spontaneous need for regulation of a systemically integrated, quasi-natural global economy and society until such time as the intermediate arena is populated by a manageable number of global players. The latter must be strong enough to form shifting coalitions, to produce a flexible system of checks and balances, and to negotiate and implement binding compromises – above all on issues of the structuring and the framing of the global ecological and economic systems. In this way, international relations as we know them would continue to exist in the transnational arena in a modified form – modified for the simple reason that under an effective UN security regime even the most powerful global players would be denied recourse to war as a legitimate means of resolving conflicts. (pp. 324–5)

On this conception, the lowest, but supporting, 'national' level of the political system of the world society would be occupied by the states which currently comprise the United Nations. Although the political constitution of these members would have to conform to the constitutional principles of the world organization, the reference to 'nation–states' suggests a false comparison with the first generation of nation–states which emerged in Europe. Moreover, it does not take account of the wide variations in the developmental paths taken by other states, which developed out of immigrant societies (USA, Australia), old empires (China), the collapse of new empires (Russia), European decolonization (India, Africa, Southeast Asia), and so forth. In the present context, the most important thing is that these nation–states, notwithstanding all of their other differences, represent the most important source of democratic legitimation for a legally constituted world society. From this follows, in particular, the requirement that the transfer of legitimation must not break off within the regional regimes. This touches upon the problem with which the European Union is primarily concerned at its current stage of development: How far must the Union assume the character of a state if it is to satisfy the standards of legitimation of its member states?

Before I examine – at least from the standpoint of conceptual consistency – whether the chain of legitimation could hold up across all levels of a politically constituted world society, I would first like to address a special legitimation problem, which follows from the denial that the world organization would assume the character of a state. In a commentary on my proposal, Rainer Schmalz-Bruns sees the core of the problem in providing 'the indispensable moments of statehood in an abstract form' for constitutionally taming a form of international politics based on violence and in 'respecifying them in contextually appropriate ways'.[9] What he means, though, is that there is a gaping hole in the proposed architecture, one which primarily concerns the legitimate expectations and demands of the citizens in their contrasting roles as *cosmopolitan* and *national* citizens. *Cosmopolitan* citizens take their orientation from universalistic standards which the peace and human rights policies of the United Nations must satisfy no less than a global domestic politics negotiated among the global players. *National* citizens, by contrast, measure the conduct of their governments and chief negotiators in these international arenas in the first instance not in accordance with *global* standards of justice, but above all in terms of the effective pursuit of *national or regional* interests. But if this conflict were fought out in the heads of the same citizens, the notions of legitimacy which evolved within the cosmopolitan framework of the international community would inevitably clash with the legitimate expectations and demands derived from the frame of reference of the respective nation–states.

116

Schmalz-Bruns appeals to an argument of Thomas Nagel, though he goes on to argue, against Nagel, that a democratic juridification of global politics can be *thought of* as possible only within a world republic, however reflexively this is structured. He quotes the following remark of Nagel:

> I believe that the newer forms of international governance share with the old a markedly indirect relation to individual citizens and that this is morally significant. All these networks bring together representatives not of individuals, but of state functions and institutions. Those institutions are responsible to their own citizens and may have to play a significant role in support of social justice for those citizens. But a global or regional network does not have a similar responsibility of social justice for the combined citizenry of all the states involved, *a responsibility that if it existed would have to be exercised collectively by the representatives of the member states.*[10]

The emphasis in the latter counterfactual conditional clause points to the key conclusion for Schmalz-Bruns, namely that the political responsibility of the national or regional governments vis-à-vis their own citizens can be relativized institutionally to the primacy of universalistic standards of justice in a political world constitution *only if the latter itself assumes the character of a state.* For only in a world state would the global political order be founded upon the will of its citizens. Only within such a framework could the democratic opinion and will formation of the citizens be organized both in a *monistic* way, as proceeding from the unity of the world citizenry, and *effectively,* and thus have binding force for implementing decisions and laws.

In response to this objection, I would like to make a differentiation. Because a politically constituted world society would be composed of citizens *and* states, the flow of legitimation produced by opinion and will formation could not proceed directly from the citizens to the

117

governing power. Instead we must take into consideration two paths of legitimation:

- the first would lead from cosmopolitan citizens, via an international community composed of member states responsive to their citizens, to the peace and human rights policy of the world organization; whereas
- the second would lead from national citizens, via a corresponding nation–state (and the relevant regional regime where one exists), to the transnational negotiation system, which would be responsible, *in the context* of the international community, for issues of global domestic policy; so that
- both paths would converge in the General Assembly of the world organization, for the latter would be responsible for the interpretation and further development of the political constitution of world society, and hence for the normative parameters both of peace and human rights policy and of global domestic politics.

2 Individuals and States as Subjects of a World Constitution

I suspect that Nagel's conceptual objection against the democratic construction of a world constitution *without a state* is informed by a misleading analogy. Applied to the constitutionalization of international law, the analogy with the social contract suggests the same construction of a 'state of nature' that served in the social contract tradition as a critical yardstick for the constitutionalization of national law. However, the *political empowerment* of a prepolitical global civil society, composed of citizens from different nations, is a different matter from *imposing a constitution* on an existing state power. In classical political theory, the thought experiment of 'leaving the state of nature', which reconstructs state power *as if* it proceeded from the rational will of free and equal individuals, was appropriate for taming the absolutist state. But, given our present dilemma, it is *not* appropriate to ignore the legitimacy of nation–states under the rule of law and to return to an original condition prior to the state. (In what follows, however, I will make a robust simplification and ignore the fact that by no means have all states developed democratic constitutions.)

Today any conceptualization of a juridification of world politics must take as its starting point individuals *and states*, as constituting the two categories of *founding subjects of a world constitution*. The (let us assume) legitimate constitutional states qualify as founding members already in virtue of their current role in guaranteeing the political self-determination of their citizens. In addition to the potential world citizens, the states represent possible sources of legitimation because patriotic citizens (in the best sense of 'patriotic'[11]) have an interest in preserving and improving the national forms of life with which they identify and for which they feel themselves responsible, though in a self-critical way, which also extends to their own national history. There is still another reason why the thought experiment of a 'second state of nature' must take into account the states as collective subjects. Where it is not a matter of *constraining* authoritarian state power but of *creating* political decision-making capabilities, those subjects who already control the legitimate means of violence and can *make them available to* a politically constituted international community are indispensable.

The thought experiment of a 'second state of nature' should satisfy three essential conditions:

(a) the contradiction between the normative standards of cosmopolitan and national citizens (analysed by Thomas Nagel) must be defused within a monistic constitutional political order;

(b) at the same time, the monistic construction should not lead to a mediatization of the world of states by the authority of a world republic which ignores the fund of trust accumulated in the domestic sphere and the associated loyalty of citizens to their respective nations; and

(c)   the deference to the distinctive national character of states and to the corresponding forms of life must not, in turn, weaken the effectiveness and the binding implementation of the supranational and transnational decisions.

(a)   In the three-level system outlined, the supranational level will be represented by a world organization which can be viewed under two aspects. In so far as the world organization enjoys the authority to intervene and regulate, it will be *specialized* in the basic functions of securing peace and protecting human rights; at the same time, however, in so far as it also embodies the international community of states and citizens as a whole, it will *represent* the *unity* of the global legal system. The Charter can play the role of a cosmopolitan constitution because it is supposed to rest both on international treaties and on domestic referenda, and hence it would be enacted 'in the name of the citizens of the states of the world' (to echo the formula employed in the European draft constitution). A General Assembly composed of representatives of the cosmopolitan citizens on the one side, and of delegates from the democratically elected parliaments of the member states on the other (or, alternatively, of one chamber for the representatives of the cosmopolitan citizens and one for the representatives of the states) would initially convene as a Constituent Assembly and subsequently assume a permanent form – within the established framework of a functionally specialized world organization – as a World Parliament, although its *legislative* function would be confined to the interpretation and elaboration of the Charter.

(b)   The General Assembly would be, among other things, the institutional locus of an inclusive formation of

opinion and will concerning the principles of transnational justice from which global domestic policy should
take its orientation. However, this discussion could not
take the form of a philosophical discussion of justice[12] for
the simple reason that it would be predetermined in a
certain sense by the composition of the General Assembly. Even in cases where representatives of the member
states and citizens of global civil society were united in a
single person, they would have to *reconcile competing
justice perspectives.* The delegates would have to combine
the task of representing the citizens of their respective
nation–states with that of safeguarding the interests of
these same citizens in their capacity as cosmopolitan citizens. The dual status of the delegates who could not
sacrifice one half of their identity to the other – or, alternatively, the establishment of a system comprising two
corresponding chambers – would prevent a priori decisions which could jeopardize the integrity of states and
the corresponding national forms of life.

In this constellation, the fundamental questions of
transnational justice would arise under *predetermined
institutional* premises. First, the inclusion of all persons in
a cosmopolitan political order would demand not only
that everyone should be accorded political and civic basic
rights, but, in addition, that the 'fair value' of these rights
should be guaranteed. This means that cosmopolitan citizens would have to be guaranteed the conditions they
require *given their respective local contexts* if they are to be
able *to make effective use* of their formally equal rights. On
this basis, fair *boundaries between national and cosmopolitan solidarity* – that is, boundaries acceptable to both sides
– would have to be laid down. This tricky problem arises
not only in the case of natural catastrophes, epidemics,
war devastation, and so on, but in the first instance regarding the mutual obligations stemming from the increasing
cooperation between states, governments, and peoples.
Such cooperation is an inevitable consequence of the
growing functional interdependence of an emerging world

society. With the inclusion of the most remote regions of the world in *the same* global economic, communications, and cultural practices, the urgent question arises of when the *particular* duties of national governments towards their own citizens – based on reciprocally recognized national borders and identities – must take a back seat to the legal obligations which the states incur towards all cosmopolitan citizens equally as members of the international community.

These obligations of the states are derived from the duties which the citizens of privileged nations have towards the citizens of disadvantaged nations, where both are considered *in their role as cosmopolitan citizens*. This kind of issue is by no means new, for similar questions also arise within individual states. When the constitution of a federal state such as Germany calls for revenue sharing among its component states and regions in order to promote 'equal living conditions', it must be assessed in which cases and respects civic solidarity can claim priority over the regional self-interest of those who live in the more productive and well-to-do states. (As it relates to individual persons as opposed to political units, the dispute in economic and social policy between liberals who want to 'ease the burdens on the productive sector' and socialists who want to stop 'redistribution from the poor to the wealthy' can be understood as a controversy concerning the primacy of civic solidarity over the particular duties of private citizens towards themselves and their dependents.)

(c)   The project of a global domestic politics without a world government leaves open the important question of who is supposed to *implement* the high-minded principles and norms agreed upon if the nation–states retain their character as states, and hence their monopoly on the use of violence. How should we imagine institutions above the state level which could ensure the implementation of a just global order while states remain states, so to speak?

The model of a multi-level system offers a different answer to this question according to the relevant policy field. Because it is supposed to secure international peace and to protect human rights, the world organization would have a hierarchical status vis-à-vis the member states. It would employ force in emergencies and draw upon the sanctioning capabilities 'lent' it by its able and willing members. According to the familiar logic of security systems – and within the framework of a suitably reformed world organization – such a practice can become established to the extent that the sovereign states learn to understand themselves also as members of the international community bound by ties of solidarity.

At the transnational level there is a growing need for coordination between functional systems which is already satisfied more or less effectively by international organizations. As we have seen, however, this holds primarily for technical questions, which can be answered by experts and do not touch upon deep-seated conflicts of interests. The situation is completely different with problems involving issues of redistribution, which call for a positive coordination of actions among the states. In issues of truly global political scope, we lack at present the necessary institutions and procedures to decide upon programs and to implement them on a broad scale. Also lacking are suitable actors who could negotiate compromises on these issues and ensure that decisions reached through fair negotiations are implemented.

3 Legitimation Requirements and Learning Processes

Having outlined the concept of a possible world order, I now want to return to our initial question concerning the conditions under which a corresponding politically constituted world society could be democratically legitimated without taking on the character of a state.

At the supranational level, a twofold need for legitima-tion arises. The negotiations and resolutions of the General Assembly, on the one hand, and the legislative, executive, and adjudicative practice of the other organs (Security Council, Secretariat, courts), on the other, must be legiti-mized. There is a qualitative difference between the need for legitimation in each case, but it can be satisfied in both only if a *functional global public sphere* emerges.[13] Vigilant civil society actors who are sensitive to relevant issues would have to lend the corresponding issues and decisions worldwide transparency and enable cosmopolitan citizens to develop informed opinions and take stances on these issues, stances which could have effects through the elec-tions to the General Assembly.

This kind of feedback would be absent in the case of the other organs of a (judicially expanded) world organi-zation which had undergone the corresponding reforms. This missing link in the chain of legitimation would have to be counterbalanced against the *nature* of the need for legitimation. The General Assembly, as the legislator under international law, (already) obeys the logic of an internal elaboration of the meaning of human rights. In so far as international politics takes its cue from this development, the resulting tasks at the supranational level would be *judicial* rather than *political* ones. To be sure, a diffuse world public opinion armed solely with the weak sanctioning power of 'naming and shaming' could exert, at best, a weak form of control over the legislative, execu-tive, and judicial decisions of the world organization. But couldn't this deficiency be made good through internal controls, namely through enhanced veto rights of the General Assembly against resolutions of the (reformed) Security Council on the one hand, and against rights of appeal from parties subject to Security Council sanctions before an International Criminal Court equipped with corresponding powers on the other?

In so far as the operation and interplay among these organs conformed to constitutional principles and procedures which reflect the results of long-running democratic learning processes, it might be acceptable that the remaining need for legitimation would be met by an informal global opinion. For the mobilizing power that an aroused global opinion acquires at critical moments in world history and transmits to governments through the channels of the national public spheres can have a major political impact, as is demonstrated by the worldwide protests against the invasion of Iraq in violation of international law. The negative duties of a universalistic morality of justice – not to commit crimes against humanity and not to conduct wars of aggression – are anchored in all cultures, and fortunately correspond to the judicially elaborated standards in terms of which the organs of the world organization would also have to justify their decisions internally. The confidence in the normative power of judicial procedures is nourished by a 'credit' of legitimation which the exemplary histories of proven democracies 'extend' to the collective memory of humankind.

The need for legitimation which would arise *at the transnational level* is of a different kind. The regulations of global domestic policy negotiated by the global players would retain an air of classic foreign policy from the perspective of the populations affected. To be sure, warmaking as a means of resolving conflicts would be prohibited; but the normative framework of the cosmopolitan constitution would prohibit the power-driven compromise formation between unequal partners from violating certain normative parameters laid down by the Charter. The *fairness* of the results could not be guaranteed completely independently of the mechanism of the balance of power – among other things, from the ability to form prudent coalitions. This does not mean that normative discourse would be excluded in favor of classic power politics at the transnational level. Power politics would no longer have the final say *within the normative framework of the international community.* The balancing of interests would take place in the transnational negotiation system *under the proviso of compliance with the parameters of justice, subject to continual adjustment in the General Assembly.* From a normative point of view, the power-driven process of compromise formation can also be understood as an application of the principles of transnational justice negotiated at the supranational level. However, 'application' should not be understood in the judicial sense of an interpretation of the law. For the principles of justice are formulated at such a high level of abstraction that the scope for discretion they leave open would have to be made good at the political level.

The democratic legitimacy of the compromises negotiated here would rest on two pillars. As in the case of international treaties, it would depend, on the one hand, on the legitimacy of the negotiating partners. The delegating powers and regional regimes would themselves have to assume a democratic character. In view of the democratic deficit that exists even in the exemplary case of the European Union, this extension of the chain of legitimation of democratic procedures beyond national borders is already an immensely ambitious requirement. On the other hand, the national public spheres would have to become responsive to one another to such a degree that transparency would be created for transnational politics within regional regimes and major powers. The delegated chief negotiators would acquire a democratic mandate at the translational level only if a process of political opinion and will formation concerning the parameters of global domestic politics took place among the citizens who were able to influence the delegating authorities.

So much for the nature of the need for legitimation. But what learning processes would be required before it could be satisfied within the institutional framework outlined? So far we have only addressed the question of conceptual coherence. But such constructions are always suspect: Are they merely naive speculations, or do they perhaps offer a way out of a concrete dilemma?

Many commentators suspect that the assumption that powerful states would make sufficient means of sanction available for the effective and impartial implementation of UN law reflects a naive underestimation of the importance of state power. This holds especially for the more far-reaching notion that the normatively constrained and pacified interplay of forces between regional regimes and major powers within the ambivalent zone between domestic and foreign policy could provide an appropriate medium for a more or less fair global domestic policy. Clearly, states and nations as we know them are still *far from* satisfying this normative expectation. Anyone who still harbored illusions concerning the strength of national power interests and the virulence of cultural conflicts has been disabused since the breach of normative constraints triggered throughout the world by the change in policy of the US government in 2001. On the other hand, an unvarnished policy of double standards is no longer accepted as normal either. This criticism, which is now widely accepted, is also justified by historical learning processes which already began in Europe and in other global regions in the post-war period.

From the perspective of a politically constituted world society, both governments and populations would have to adopt new orientations and, in this sense, 'learn'. Of course, it is easier for smaller states exposed to the full force of the imperatives of an increasingly globalized economy and to the pressures to cooperate being exerted by an increasingly complex world society to internalize the norms of the world organization. They find it easier than the major powers to come to see themselves as members of the international community and as co-players in international organizations without formally renouncing their monopoly on the means of violence.

The de facto development is also reflected at the normative level of the evolution of basic concepts in international law. The classic meaning of 'sovereignty' has already shifted in a direction anticipated by Hans Kelsen.

127

Today the sovereign state is supposed to operate as a fallible agent of the world community; under the threat of sanctions, its task is to guarantee that all citizens enjoy equal human rights in the guise of basic legal rights within its national borders. The conception of legal validity, which hitherto took its cue from positive and 'coercive' national law, is also undergoing a tacit change. In so far as the competences to set and implement law no longer reside in the same hands, an essential presupposition of this conception is no longer fulfilled. In this regard the European Union, with its division of labor between supranational and national levels, provides an instructive example. While the central institutions enact European law, the member states, although they retain the monopoly of the legitimate means of violence, are bound to – and in fact do – implement the decisions of the European authorities without demur. Since this pattern works in other sectors of international law too, the gap in the dimension of legal validity or degree of bindingness between international law and national law is already narrowing.

The other learning process concerns peoples rather than their governments, namely, overcoming an obstinate mindset historically bound up with the evolution of the nation–state. In the course of the regional amalgamation of nation–states into empowered global actors, national consciousness, and thus the existing basis of an already highly abstract form of civic solidarity, would have to undergo a further extension. A mobilization of masses along religious, ethnic, or nationalistic lines will become less likely the more the demands for tolerance of a pluralistic civic ethos are already accepted within national borders. In this sense, the development of a European 'identity' can be understood as the continuation of a process which is already taking place within some of the member states. In response to challenging historical experiences, and as immigrant groups who maintain ties to their countries of origin become culturally and politically

128

integrated, there are already initial signs of a properly understood constitutional patriotism as a basis for civic integration within these states.

Thus far, the national governments have been the pace-makers in the treaty-based construction of new legal relations which function like a self-fulfilling prophecy when they trigger new practices and give rise to self-sustaining patterns of action. This kind of law-making often antici-pates the transformation in mentalities which occurs among the addressees only as the laws and question are gradually implemented. This holds equally for the politi-cal elites and for the citizens. This hypothesis concerning the socializing effects of imposed legal norms also accounts for Antje Wiener's finding that the national elites who go to 'Brussels' or 'Strasbourg' have a more 'European' mindset than those who remain in their national bases.[14] The implications of a legal change in status, which is for-mally accepted to begin with, permeate the consciousness of the broader population only as a result of practical experiences. For example, European citizenship first acquires concrete significance through the practice of entering and exiting foreign countries within Europe and outside Europe.

The image of a mentally lethargic population 'lagging behind' the political elites in the process of enlargement represents just one side of the coin. Once elites decide to make existential questions such as the adoption of a Euro-pean constitution the focus of a wide-ranging, informed public debate, a population can also overtake its govern-ment. One explanation for the 'unpredictability' of refer-enda is that a politically mobilized population can make decisions without concern for professional politicians' interest in retaining power. For example, the 'European enthusiasm' of national elites dwindles once their own powers and opportunities for self-promotion are placed in question along with the scope for action of national gov-ernments – with the role of the French or the German foreign minister, for example, or with the importance of the French president, the German chancellor, or the British prime minister. The peculiar dialectical relation between the learning processes of populations and those of governments suggests that, for example, the impasse in the development of the European Union following the failure of two referenda, which the Lisbon Treaty does not really solve, cannot be overcome through the usual intergovernmental agreements.

8
Media, Markets and Consumers: The Quality Press as the Backbone of the Political Public Sphere

This April the business section of *Die Zeit* startled its readers with the headline 'Will the Fourth Estate come under the hammer?'[1] The article was prompted by the alarming news that the *Süddeutsche Zeitung* is facing an uncertain economic future because a majority of the owners want to sell their shares. If it should come to an auction, one of Germany's two leading national newspapers could fall into the hands of finance investors, listed companies, or large media concerns. Others will say: business as usual. What is so alarming about owners making use of their right to sell their shares, for whatever reason?

Like other newspapers, the *Süddeutsche Zeitung* has by now overcome the crisis triggered by the collapse in the advertising market in early 2002. The families who control more than 62 percent of the shares and now want to disinvest have chosen an opportune moment. Profits are rising, in spite of competition from the digital sector and changing readership habits. However, this is mainly due to rationalization measures which affect levels of performance and the freedom of the editorial departments. Related reports concerning the American newspaper sector confirm this trend.

The Boston Globe, for instance, one of the few left-liberal newspapers in the country, has had to cut back on all of its foreign correspondents. The flagships of the national press, such as *The Washington Post*, *The New York Times*, and *The Los Angeles Times*, fear takeovers by companies or funds with unreasonable profit expectations which want to 'streamline' these exacting media. Then last week *Die Zeit* published a second article on the 'battle of Wall Street financial managers against the US press'.[2] What is behind such headlines? Clearly it is the apprehension that the markets on which the national newspapers must compete today cannot perform the dual function hitherto performed by the quality press, namely that of satisfying the demand for information and education while generating a profit.

The Objection of Paternalism

But don't higher profits confirm that 'downsized' newspaper companies are satisfying the wishes of their readers? Don't vague terms like 'professional', 'demanding', and 'serious' simply camouflage a patronizing attitude towards consumers who know perfectly well what they want? May the press restrict the freedom of choice of their readers under the pretext of 'quality'? May it force them to read dry reports instead of infotainment, and try their patience with factual commentaries and complex arguments instead of more accessible stories on people and events?

The objection underlying these questions is plausible only at first sight. It rests upon the controversial assumption that customers make independent decisions in accordance with their preferences. This piece of schoolbook wisdom is certainly misleading, bearing in mind the special character of the commodity 'cultural and political communication'. For this commodity also puts the preferences of its consumers to the test. To be sure, readers, listeners, and viewers are guided by different preferences in using the media. They want to be entertained or distracted, to be informed about certain issues and processes, or to participate in public discussions. But as soon as they open themselves to cultural or political programs, for example by receiving Hegel's 'realistic morning blessing' through daily newspaper reading, they expose themselves to an 'auto-paternalistic' learning process whose outcome is indefinite. Only over many years of reading do they form new preferences, convictions, and value-orientations. The meta-preference which guides such a reading takes its cue from the merits expressed in the professional self-image of independent journalism which underlie the reputation of the quality press.

The Example of Television

This dispute over the special character of the commodities of education and information is reminiscent of a slogan that made the rounds as television was being introduced into the United States: this medium, it was said, is nothing more than 'a toaster with pictures'. By this it was meant that the production and consumption of television programs could safely be left to the market. Since then, media enterprises have produced programs for viewers and sold the attention of their audience to advertisers. This organizational principle has inflicted widespread political and cultural damage wherever it became the dominant model. In the German case, this damage has been held in check by a 'dual' private–public television system. At any rate, the media laws of the German states, the relevant judgments of the Federal Constitutional Court, and the programming guidelines of the public broadcasters reflect the view that the electronic mass media should not only satisfy the more marketable needs for entertainment and distraction of consumers.

Radio and television audiences are not only consumers, that is, market participants, but also citizens who have a right to partake in culture, to follow political events, and to be involved in the formation of political opinions. Given this legal entitlement, the channels which supply the

133

population's basic needs in this area must not be made dependent on their advertising effectiveness or on the support of sponsors. At the same time, the officially fixed license fees which finance these basic needs in Germany should not be contingent on states' budgetary situations, hence on the ups and downs of the economy. The broadcasting corporations justifiably cite this argument in proceedings between them and the state governments currently pending before the Federal Constitutional Court.[3]

The Role of the Leading Media ...

Now, a protected public legal status may be all well and good in the case of the role of the electronic media. But can it provide a model in an emergency for organizing 'serious' newspapers and magazines such as the *Süddeutsche Zeitung*, the *Frankfurter Allgemeine*, *Die Zeit*, or *Der Spiegel*? A result of studies conducted by communication researchers is of interest here. At least in the domain of political communication – in other words, for the readers as citizens – the quality press plays the role of 'leading media'. Even radio and television, as well as to the remainder of the press, depend to a large extent on the issues and reports fed to them by the 'reasoning' newspapers in their political reporting and commentary.

What if some of these papers were to come under pressure from financial investors with an inappropriate short-term outlook, in search of a quick profit? Were reorganization and cost-cutting in this core area to jeopardize customary journalistic standards, it would strike at the very heart of the public sphere. For without the inflow of information gained through extensive research, and without the stimulus of arguments based on an expertise that doesn't come cheap, political communication would lose its discursive vitality. The public sphere would no longer offer any resistance to populist tendencies and would be incapable of performing its proper function in a constitutional democracy.

We live in pluralistic societies. The democratic decision-making process can overcome deep differences in outlooks only as long as it gives rise to a legitimate bonding force which is convincing to all citizens and satisfies a combination of two requirements: it must combine inclusion, that is, the equal participation of all citizens, with a more or less discursively conducted conflict of opinions. For only deliberative conflicts support the supposition that the democratic procedure will lead to more or less reasonable results in the long run. The formation of democratic opinion and will has an epistemic dimension, because it also involves criticism of false assertions and value judgments. The discursive vitality of the public sphere plays a role in this process. One can get an intuitive idea of this from the difference between competing public opinions and from the publication of the distributions of opinions established by opinion polls. Public opinions produced through discussion and polemics, however conflicting, have already been filtered through the relevant information and argumentation, whereas opinion polls merely reflect 'latent' opinions in their raw and dormant state.

... in Democratic Opinion and Will Formation

Of course, the unchanneled flows of communication of a public sphere dominated by the mass media preclude the kind of regulated discussion or consultation that one finds in the law courts or parliamentary committees. But the latter is not necessary either, because the public sphere is just one link in a chain. It mediates between the institutionalized discourses and negotiations in the state arenas on the one hand, and the episodic and informal everyday conversations of potential voters on the other. The public sphere plays its part in democratically legitimizing state

135

action by selecting the matters which are relevant for political decision-making, reworking them into statements of problems and aggregating them into competing public opinions through more or less well-informed and reasoned arguments.

In this way, public communication is a force which both stimulates and orients citizens' opinions and desires, while at the same time compelling the political system to adapt and become more transparent. The public sphere can no longer infuse this special type of energy without the impulses from an influential press, which provides reliable information and conscientious commentary. When it comes to gas, electricity, or water, the state has an obligation to ensure the energy supply for the population. Shouldn't it have a similar obligation when it comes to supplying this other type of 'energy', whose interruption causes disruptions harmful to the democratic state itself? There is no question of a 'system failure' when the state tries to protect the public good of the quality press in a particular case. It is just a pragmatic question of how this can be best done.

No Experiments?

In the past, the government of the state of Hessen bailed out the *Frankfurter Rundschau* with a loan – to no avail. But one-off subsidies are just one mechanism. Others are foundations with public involvement, or tax breaks for family holdings in this sector. These experiments have already been tried elsewhere, and none of them is unproblematic. But we first need to get used to the idea that newspapers and magazines should be subsidized. From a historical point of view, there is something counterintuitive in the notion of reining in the market's role in journalism and in the press. The market first provided the stage on which subversive ideas could emancipate themselves from state repression. Yet the market can play this role only as long as economic constraints do not permeate the cultural and political contents disseminated via the market. This remains the kernel of truth in Adorno's criticism of the culture industry. Vigilance is required, because no democracy can afford a market failure in this sector.

9
Political Communication in Media Society: Does Democracy still have an Epistemic Dimension? The Impact of Normative Theory on Empirical Research*

In memoriam Bernhard Peters

Normative theorizing and empirical research go hand in hand in Aristotle's *Politics*. Today political theories in the social contract tradition express an abstract 'ought' which clashes with sobering facts in our increasingly complex societies. This seems to be especially true of the deliberative model of democracy, which explicates the legitimacy-conferring power of the democratic procedure in terms of the rational character of opinion and will formation. This model seems to constitute a particularly drastic example of the ever-widening gap between normative and empirical approaches towards politics. In the early days of Paul Lazarsfeld's radio research, the connection between communication studies – or what was then known as the 'dominant paradigm' – and the search for the roots of popular democracy in mass societies was still apparent.[1] But how does a normatively loaded conception of 'deliberative politics' cohere with our supposedly realistic image of the media society?[2]

*A shorter version was presented at the opening of the World Congress of the International Communication Association in Dresden in June 2006.

I will begin by comparing the deliberative with the liberal and the republican models of democracy and establish possible links to empirical research (I). I will then go on to examine whether there is empirical evidence for the assumption that political discourses deal with questions which are, in principle, rationally decidable and that they have a truth-tracking potential (II). The three central parts of the paper will serve to dispel *prima facie* doubts concerning the empirical content and applicability of the deliberative model. Clearly, mass communication does not correspond to the picture of spontaneous and reciprocal face-to-face communication, which seems to provide the model for 'deliberation' (III). If we consider the legitimation process as a whole and examine the interrelations between the political system and society at large, however, neither the structure nor the power dynamics of political communication in the mass media pose insurmountable obstacles to the formation of rationally filtered, and in this sense 'considered', public opinions (IV and V). However, the model of communication which I will develop for deliberative politics must satisfy two key conditions: media-based political communication can promote deliberative legitimation processes in the public spheres of complex societies only in so far as, first, a self-regulating media system becomes independent of its social environment and, second, the diffuse mass audience – that is, the readers, the listeners, and the viewers of mass media – produce a feedback relation between the informed elite discourses and a responsive civil society (VI). With the legitimation deficit of the new forms of governance beyond the nation–state in mind, I will conclude with some remarks on the rise of transnational public spheres (VII).

I Three Normative Theories of Democracy and their Empirical References

The institutional design of modern democracies combines three elements: the private autonomy of citizens, each one of whom has the right to pursue a life of her own; democratic citizenship, that is, the uniform inclusion of free and equal citizens in the political community; and an independent public sphere, which functions as an intermediary domain between state and society and in which citizens form opinions and desires. The functional separation between the administrative state and a capitalist economy explains why modern societies with democratic constitutions depend on the mediating functions of a public space which is responsive to the spontaneous inputs and stances of the citizens. Everywhere, these three elements constitute the normative substance of liberal governments, irrespective of the differences between constitutional texts, legal orders, political institutions, and practices. In what follows I will confine myself to these elements.

The design of the constitution guarantees (1) the legal protection of the private sphere through

- a system of equal basic liberties for all the citizens which is compatible with the same liberties for everybody (Kant's legal principle);
- equal access to, and legal protection by, independent courts; and
- the separation of powers between the legislative, judicial, and executive branches, which binds public administration to the law.

The design of the constitution guarantees (2) the political participation of as many interested citizens as possible through

- equal rights of association, participation, and communication for all;
- periodic elections and, if necessary, referenda based on universal suffrage;
- competition between different parties, platforms, and programs; and

140

- the majority principle for political decisions in representative bodies.

The design of the constitution guarantees (3) an appropriate contribution of a public sphere to the formation of considered public opinions through

- a separation between the tax-gathering state and a market-based society (where the principle of guaranteeing individual economic liberties does not imply a prior commitment to a neoliberal form of economic organization);
- freedom of the press, diversity of the mass media, and freedom of information; and
- regulations guaranteeing mass audiences and civil society access to the public sphere and preventing the monopolization of arenas of public communication by political, social, or economic interests.

Although these three elements – equal liberties, democratic participation, and government by public opinion – are fused into a single design within the family of constitutional states, they are accorded different relative weights in different traditions. The liberal tradition reveals a preference for the liberties of private citizens, whereas the republican and the deliberative traditions stress the political participation of active citizens in the democratic process and in the formation of considered public opinions, respectively.[3]

The liberal tradition, which can be traced back in essence to John Locke and was a major source of inspiration for the American founding fathers, focuses on the first element, namely the legal institutionalization of human rights, and in particular of the negative rights celebrated as the 'Freedoms of the Moderns'. The intuition informing this still dominant line of political thought is that private persons in their natural social habitat must be shielded from the interventions of an intrusive state power. The essential role of the constitutional state is to protect individuals who

141

wish to pursue their own highly personal life plans. The primary emphasis is on taming public power through the rule of law, and the democratic process is accorded a relatively modest function. On the liberal conception, political rights give the citizens the opportunity to promote their private interests in such a way that these can in the end be aggregated into a political force which influences the administration through elections, through the composition of parliamentary bodies, and through the choice of a government.

This instrumentalist conception of democracy contrasts sharply with the republican ethics of citizenship, in which the pathos of national self-determination finds expression. The republican tradition, which was revived by Renaissance humanism and influenced the American Revolution through James Harrington and, especially, the French Revolution through Jean-Jacques Rousseau, focuses on the second element, namely on renewing the 'Freedoms of the Ancients' under the modern social conditions of a functionally differentiated society. It is a response to the fear that involvement in the business life of modern market societies cuts citizens off from political life. The intuition which informs this line of thought is expressed in the principle of popular sovereignty. Governmental power should not be merely codified in law and subordinated to the interests of the citizens of a prepolitically constituted society. On the republican conception, the power of the state, which proceeds from the people and continually justifies and reproduces itself through the democratic process, is constitutive instead of social life at large. Here the construction of the constitutional state is conceived in terms of the goal of facilitating a practice of self-determination which is conducted jointly by the united citizenry and not, as in the liberal tradition, with a view to facilitating each individual's autonomous conduct of life. The citizens must not confuse their political rights with the negative rights they claim as private persons. The status of the citizen oriented to the common good should not be assimilated to that of consumers or clients who pursue their private interests alone.

The third element, the freedom to express one's opinion in public deliberations, which functions as a transmission belt between civil society and the deliberative and decision-making institutions of the state, was a source of inspiration for nineteenth-century parliamentary movements in particular. Kant and the liberals of the *Vormärz* in Germany and Switzerland (Welcker and Rotteck, Julius Fröbel) made important contributions to this tradition, as did John Stuart Mill and, with different arguments, John Dewey. Granted, the deliberative paradigm has had less impact on the history of political ideas than classical liberalism or republicanism. Nevertheless, given the revolution in electronic communication, the deliberative paradigm[4] is well suited to relating the strong normative ideas to present-day social complexity in such a way that they are not frustrated from the outset by countervailing facts. (That, at any rate, was my aim in the contributions to the discourse theory of law and constitutional democracy developed in *Between Facts and Norms*.[5])

The deliberative model conceives of the public sphere as a sounding board for registering problems which affect society as a whole, and at the same time as a discursive filter-bed which sifts interest-generalizing and informative contributions to relevant topics out of the unregulated processes of opinion formation, broadcasts these 'public opinions' back onto the dispersed public of citizens, and puts them on the formal agendas of the responsible bodies. For the republican model, the democratic process has the expressive status of an articulation of will; and for the liberal model it performs the function of binding the policies of the government to the rational self-interest of private citizens. For the deliberative model, by contrast, embedding the will of the electorate and the formal procedures of deliberation and decision-making in the vibrant and maximally unregulated circulation of public opinions exerts a rationalizing pressure towards improving the *quality* of the decisions.

Thus the deliberative model is more concerned with the reasonableness of discourses and negotiations than with the fair aggregation of the motives of success-oriented individuals or with the authentic character of the common will of a nation. Here the cooperative search for shared solutions to problems takes the place of the aggregated interests of private individuals or of the collective ethos of the citizen body. The procedures and communicative presuppositions of the formation of democratic opinion and will serve as the most important sluices for the discursive rationalization of the decisions of the government and of the administration. *Rationalization*, in this context, means more than just legitimation, though less than the constitution of power. The aggregate condition of administrative power changes when it is fed back into a process of discursive opinion and will formation; of course, the communicative power into which democratic procedures process the competition of public opinions cannot itself 'govern', but can at most influence the way administrative power is used.

Thus a cursory glance at the history of political ideas reveals the *three different perspectives* from which the *same* institutional complex continues to be perceived. These three modes of perception and interpretation shape the self-understanding of citizens, politicians, administrators, and hence also the dominant practices of making and applying the law within a political community with a liberal constitution – practices which determine both the political identity of a population and the political culture of the country.[6] Aristotle was aware that the 'ordinary' citizens of a polity are the natural addressees of political theory. With his conception of an 'overlapping consensus', John Rawls even incorporated this direct relation between theory and practice into the theory itself, as a self-reflexive element.[7] Another, more indirect way of establishing a connection between normative theory and political reality is to implement such a theory in designs for empirical research in the corresponding fields of political science.[8]

This explains the elective affinities between political liberalism and the economic theory of democracy on one side, republicanism and certain communitarian approaches to research on democracy on the other. The liberal conception of democracy takes the rule of law as its starting point and focuses on the legal institutionalization of the liberties of the citizens in a market society. Accordingly, the economic theory of democracy views political processes from the standpoint of rational choice and explains the democratic process through the competition between parties based on the enlightened self-interest of the citizens.[9] The republican conception of democracy turns on the idea of popular sovereignty and establishes an empirical connection between the self-determination of the citizens and their political ethos. The corresponding research programs in political science and sociology deal with issues of a liberal political culture, appropriate forms of political socialization, or other sources of solidarity (e.g. trust or 'habits of the heart') as functional requirements for stabilizing democratic regimes.[10]

Whereas the narrow perspective on citizen commitment of an ethics of liberal citizenship fails to take account of the enormous complexity of modern political systems, rational choice explanations suppress essential normative features of political conduct. The deliberative model focuses on the reasonableness of discourses and negotiations rather than on rational choice or on the political ethos.[11] Here the cooperative search for solutions to political problems by deliberating citizens takes the place of the preference-aggregation of private citizens underlying competitive models of democracy or of the collective self-determination of a normatively integrated nation.

II The Truth-Tracking Potential of Political Deliberation

The main empirical reference of the deliberative model is a democratic process which is ascribed a power to generate legitimacy on the basis of certain procedural characteristics.[12] If the democratic procedure of opinion and will formation is to lead to legitimate decisions, it must be so constituted that the supposition of the equal inclusion of all those possibly affected and the prospect of reasonable outcomes (also in virtue of rational preference change) is justified.

In the present context I must ignore certain aspects in order to concentrate on the contribution of the public sphere to legitimation. The important connection between the democratic *legitimation* of political authority and the political *integration* of the citizens becomes apparent only under the aspect of a legally generated, and hence abstract, civic solidarity. I must likewise set aside the controversial relation between argumentation and negotiation (that is, between discursive will formation and compromise),[13] as well as the coupling of discourses with decision-making procedures that measure up to the rationally motivating power of arguments.[14] In contrast to the institutionalized deliberations of courts, parliaments, committees, or cabinet meetings, the rationalizing power of the public sphere should extend only to the formation of opinions, not to political decisions. Of course, the rational expectations built into the deliberative model are geared to the process of legitimation *as a whole*.

I would first like to explain the concept of 'epistemic proceduralism' and the corresponding research paradigm (1), before I go on to cite some relevant examples from empirical studies (2).

(1) Rational discourses call for the spontaneous and reciprocal exchange of reasons for informed positions on relevant topics and inputs. The guiding idea of the model of deliberative politics is that the formation of political will is channeled through the filter of discursive opinion formation. This conception ascribes a cognitive function to the democratic process in so far as the latter, *taken as a whole*, satisfies the conditions which are necessary, first,

to guarantee the inclusion of all those affected, the transparency of the deliberation, and that everyone has an equal chance to participate; and, second, to justify the assumption that the democratic process will lead to reasonable results.

This supposition rests in turn on the assumption that suitably institutionalized deliberations can approximately fulfill the functions of (a) mobilizing relevant lines of enquiry, topics, and claims, requisite information, and suitable arguments for and against; and (b) evaluating these contributions at an explanatory level appropriate to the problem, so that the 'yes' and 'no' stances are rationally motivated (and hence are reasonable, having come about without deception and violence) and shape the results of procedurally correct decisions.

Of course, we must take into account the fact that in complex political systems the democratic process unfolds in a variety of different arenas involving different communicative settings and functions. Only from the perspective of the functional *division of labor between the arenas* is it reasonable to expect that the system *as a whole* will fulfill the presumed epistemic functions of a discursive process of opinion and will formation. This expectation loses its excessively utopian appearance once we recognize the *everyday roots* of the intuitive expectation that communicative actors in favorable communicative settings can clarify controversial validity claims, learn from one another, and jointly solve problems.

Arguments are, no doubt, pretty demanding forms of communication. However, they grow out of the daily routines of giving and asking for reasons. In the course of everyday communication, the actors are always already moving within a 'space of reasons'. As soon as they want to reach a communicative understanding with one another, participants *cannot fail to* raise mutual validity claims for their utterances. In doing so they implicitly claim that what they say can be accepted as true or right or truthful, or in any case as reasonable, and that, if what they say is placed in question, it can be rationally justified in these respects.[15] In this trivial sense, a reference to discourses, to the competition for better arguments, is already *implicit* in our routine behavior as an omnipresent alternative. Thus ideas enter into social reality via *unavoidable idealizing presuppositions* of everyday practices and unobtrusively acquire the character of stubborn social facts.[16]

Political practices and legally regulated procedures operate under similar presuppositions. Take the example of the so-called voter's paradox (in which I can find nothing paradoxical). In general, citizens are not discouraged from participating in elections by what political scientists report, from an observer's point of view, about the neutralizing effects of voting procedures and of electoral geography. For citizens, the democratic practice of voting has the meaning of a collective enterprise which functions only on the assumption that every vote 'counts' and carries equal weight. In their role as *participants* in this practice, the citizens are not bothered when political scientists assure them of the contrary from the *observer* perspective. Likewise, litigants do not stop going to court to 'seek justice', irrespective of what law professors or other experts tell them about the indeterminacy of laws and the unpredictability of legal decisions. The administration of justice – indeed the rule of law in general – would break down if those involved ceased to act on the tacit assumption that they receive fair treatment and a reasonable verdict.

Of course, such implicit presuppositions, which are *unavoidably* linked with the performance of certain practices, should not be confused with empirical predictions. But practices such as communicative action, democratic voting, or bringing a case before the court could not function unless the participants tacitly attributed to them some inherent cognitive or even 'truth-tracking' potential. Adequate accounts of such practices in the social sciences, therefore, must also incorporate these *counterfactual suppositions*, for example procedural standards which the participants regard as valid or assume to be 'followed' and

148

'fulfilled'. The deliberative research paradigm calls for a methodology which takes into account the counterfactual content of such presuppositions. Neither the methodological individualism of rational choice theory nor the normal hermeneutic procedures of communitarian accounts suffice for the kind of epistemic proceduralism I advocate. The hermeneutic access to intersubjectively shared practices must instead be combined with the rational reconstruction of the cognitive potential inherent in these practices.

The reconstruction of tacitly assumed counterfactual presuppositions yields an independent standard of evaluation, which is rooted in those observed practices themselves. Thus, for example, the normative constraints to which democratic opinion and will formation is subject – the equal inclusion of those affected and the discursive quality of the opinion and will formation itself – can be read off from the counterfactual content of what the participants themselves presuppose when they view the outcomes of a democratic procedure as legitimate even if they do not agree with them. Since 'assumed fulfillment' is not the same thing as actual fulfillment, there is an observable difference between valid claims and those assumed to be valid. It is an interesting empirical question at what point perceived differences of this kind are no longer accepted as 'normal' but exceed a threshold beyond which the participants feel alienated from an established practice.

(2)   Of course, it is an empirical question whether rational discourses are to be found in the field *of political communication*. I would like to illustrate this with some examples from small group research. These studies conceive of political communication as a mechanism for enhancing cooperative learning and problem-solving.[17] Michael A. Neblo has translated basic assumptions of discourse theory into empirically testable hypotheses and has examined, using issues such as the fairness of tax schemes, affirmative action, and 'gays in the military', whether discourses can foster learning processes in experimental groups.[18]

The test persons were first asked individually about their opinions on these issues; five weeks later they took part in group discussions on the same issues, with the request to reach collective decisions if possible; and after a further five weeks they were each asked again for their individual opinions. The findings more or less confirm the hypotheses concerning the positive impact of deliberation on the formation of considered opinions. The final opinions differed considerably from those expressed at the outset. The group deliberations tended to promote a convergence rather than a polarization of opinions. Afterwards the participants exhibited improved levels of information and, in general, wider perspectives and had a more comprehensive and precise definition of the issues. In the end, arguments which counted independently of the person of the speaker outweighed the influence of interpersonal relations, and the interviewees' trust in argumentation as a problem-solving procedure increased.

If we order the relevant group studies on a scale extending from experimental studies to field research, James Fishkin's famous experiments with focus groups are next in line.[19] In these experiments, representative samples of citizen groups were invited to participate in an informal voting procedure on some controversial public policy issue. A period of study and informal conversations concerning the relevant briefing materials, including major arguments for and against pending legislative proposals, was followed by a weekend of deliberation in small groups, led by trained moderators. Whereas Neblo's experimental groups – or, to take another example, the 160 voters from British Columbia drawn at random from voters' lists for a Citizen's Assembly on Electoral Reform, who were informed about alternative pending electoral reform proposals over six weekends and were supposed to reach decisions after exhaustive discussions[20] – were engaged in *collective* decision-making processes, Fishkin's test persons were questioned as voters, a role where what ultimately counts is each participant's individual opinion.

Although in the latter case rational decision-making was studied only under the aspect of the 'weighing of preferences', the group discussions prompted the participants to acquire adequate information, weigh substantive arguments, and broaden the scope of their reflections. The measured effects involved increases in knowledge and unidirectional changes of opinion, so that the differences can be interpreted as effects of learning. Following deliberation, votes depend more on normatively desirable criteria and less on preferences predictable in the light of social, educational, and demographic backgrounds. Another cognitive gain is a better grasp of the point at issue, in other words, understanding what is really at stake. Improved understanding of analytical viewpoints – better values in the dimension of 'single-peakedness' – leads to the clarification of the relevant aspects under which one can argue for or against a position or a validity claim.

The empirical data concerning the influence of arguments on the formation of preferences have not only led to a wider discussion of the limits of the rational choice approach.[21] They have also led to new research on so-called framing effects, that is, the effects of interpretive perspectives on the formation of political preferences. Thus it has been established that discourses prompt participants to make considered comparisons between different, competing interpretive frames, and thus to counter unreflective framing effects;[22] in the process, the positive, eye-opening effects of surprising interpretations also becomes apparent. Rhetoric owes its Janus face to the world-disclosing power of new vocabularies as much as to the constraining, often manipulative effects of suggestive and emotionally charged metaphors.[23]

Closer to real-life politics were the mediation groups composed of experts (from multinational corporations) and counter-experts (from non-governmental organizations) brought together by the Berlin Wissenschaftszentrum under the direction of Wolfgang van den Daele. These discussion groups met to discuss their conflicting views on pressing issues such as the risks involved in intro-ducing genetically modified plant species, or the impact of medical patents on combating epidemics in the afflicted regions of Africa.[24] In this instance, an active moderator was supposed to ensure a certain level of discussion by laying down topics in advance, structuring contributions, seeking clarifications, and ensuring that the rules of argu-mentation were observed. Although the conflicting positions of the opposed 'camps' did not permit a rap-prochement concerning vested interests and basic values, the 'force of the better argument' nevertheless had a striking impact. Once again, there were measurable effects in the increase in information, in the conceptual clarifica-tion of controversial issues, in the reduction of disagree-ment, and in the willingness to learn from one another. Unacknowledged errors and misleading interpretations were quietly withdrawn, and dogmatic prejudices receded into the background over the course of the deliberations.

III Deliberation and Mass Communication

Studies such as these yield empirical evidence for the assumption that political deliberation has a cognitive poten-tial. However, because of their small group format, such studies can provide, at best, limited information concern-ing the usefulness of a deliberative research design for the graduated and complex processes of legitimation in large-scale national societies. In contemporary western societies, on which I will concentrate in what follows, we can observe an impressive concentration and diversification of political communication.[25] But the public sphere is at the same time inundated by the kind of media-based mass communica-tion which is almost devoid of deliberative characteristics.

The progressive functional differentiation of societal subsystems, the growing diversity of interests, and the pluralism of worldviews and cultural forms of life account for the increasing complexity of the matters in need of regulation over which politics claims jurisdiction. This complexity requires an increasing mass of formal and informal exchanges, discussions, negotiations, compromises, arbitration processes, and so on at all stages of the political process. Ever more communication is required to coordinate and adjust conflicting demands on the input side, to formulate programs and corresponding decisions within the political system, and to implement them on the output side. Political elites operate under the watchful gaze of the media and of their distrustful audiences, while at the same time anxiously tracking shifts in public opinion and in the polls in order to be able to respond to them. The inflated volume of messages, ideas, and images in circulation creates at least the impression that contemporary politics is becoming ever more deeply entangled in processes of mass communication, indeed that it is being assimilated into and transformed by them.

The impression of a *communicative liquefaction of politics* is bound up with three interdependent macro-developments, which underline the political relevance of communication networks and have prompted sociologists to speak in terms of an 'information', 'network', and 'media' society.[26] These labels refer, respectively, to the rise of an information economy; to the concentration and acceleration of information flows already alluded to; and to the revolution in information technologies.

A distinctive feature of post-industrial societies is a shift in the composition of the workforce from the industrial to the service sector. Corresponding changes in the education system are leading to an increase in the number of well-educated individuals who are trained to absorb and process complex information. People at all levels of society are being exposed to accelerated information flows,[27] although access to new media and the ability to cope with the information overload are still extremely unequally distributed between the rich and the poor, men and women, and the better-educated and less well-educated classes and countries.[28] The most striking among these trends is a continuous series of technological innovations, beginning with the telephone and extending, via radio and television, to fax and the Internet. This revolution in the media for transmitting information has given rise to an ever-wider spread and density of communication networks and to a corresponding diversification of the mass public.[29]

However, these phenomenological indicators of an inflation in political communication and of a communicative liquefaction of politics do not of themselves speak for an upsurge of deliberative politics. Rhetorical and for the most part non-discursive modes of expression such as story-telling and images, facial and bodily expressions in general, testimonies, appeals, and the like are in any case normal parts of political communication. But the kind of mass communication which is channeled through the print and through the electronic media lacks, above all, the procedural constraints to which face-to-face negotiations in political institutions such as courts or parliamentary committees are subject. The kind of media-based mass communication with which we are familiar from national public spheres is not subject to any standards of discursive quality, or even representativeness. In virtue of its structure alone, it lacks certain characteristic features of a discursive dispute. In comparison to institutionalized opinion and will formation, two deficits in particular stand out: the lack of straightforward, face-to-face interactions, between really (or virtually) present participants, in a shared practice of collective decision-making; and the lack of reciprocity between the roles of speakers and addressees in an egalitarian exchange of opinions and claims. In addition, the *dynamics of mass communication* betrays relations of power which make a mockery of the presumption of a free play of arguments. The power of the media to select messages and to shape their presentation is as much an intrinsic feature of mass communication as the fact that other actors use their power to influence the agenda, content, and presentation of public issues is typical of the public sphere. Whereas the latter defect is a rather contingent feature which depends on how political and social power is distributed and regulated within a specific society at a particular time, the other features are inherent traits of mass communication.

But must we understand these deviations of mass communication from the model of discursive disputes as defects at all? In view of the function that the public sphere is supposed to play in the graduated legitimation process of a constitutional democracy, it is by no means a foregone conclusion that the *abstract* and *asymmetrical* structure or the power-steered dynamics of mass communication is necessarily a disadvantage. Before I address the power dynamics, I will first focus on the two structural features of mass communication that deviate from the mode of communication of face-to-face discourses.

The abstract spatial structure of the public sphere can be understood as an extension of the kind of social spaces which are created in face-to-face interactions. National public spheres find embodiment in networks through which the 'wild', that is, by and large unorganized, intermingling streams of information flow. These networks transmit messages of different kinds: news bulletins and reports, opinions and essays, commentaries and moderated discussions, cabarets, shows, films, images, and productions – in short, entertaining, instructive, or even edifying programs and informative, educational, or dramatic broadcasts. These messages are produced and presented by the media (or by institutions such as theatres, museums, libraries, and so on); are broadcast through local or national networks; are received and consumed by different sorts of readers, listeners, viewers, and visitors; and are taken up and commented upon by interest groups, parties, camps, subcultures, and so on.

Political public spheres transmit a confused din of voices; however they do not merely disseminate but also exercise a centripetal force. They condense 'public opinions' out of flows of political messages. These can be understood as syntheses of innumerable, topic-specific stances taken by a diffuse mass public on more or less well-defined public problems and inputs. Thus it is not the case that mass communication is insensitive to the resonance generated by the broader public; otherwise the public sphere could not play the role of a sounding board for society-wide problems – a role which it is supposed to assume on the liberal model.[30] But mass communication remains 'abstract' in so far as it disregards the actual presence of the more or less passive recipients and ignores the immediateness of the concrete glances, gestures, thoughts, and reactions of those who are present and addressed.

Mass communication is not open to the game of direct question and answer, to the exchange of affirmation and negation, assertion and contradiction, among those present. It does not seem to bear any resemblance to simple interactions in which the participants share practical and communicative goals, but it is more like a price-regulated network of transactions between producers and consumers. Whereas deliberation in the process of forming political opinion and will promotes the shared purpose of finding legitimate solutions to divisive problems, the massive streams of opinions that surge through the public sphere seem to be detached from collective learning and decision-making. Disconnected from face-to-face interaction, the propositional contents begin to float free from the binding force of reciprocal validity claims. Once opinions degenerate into *mere* opinions, there is nothing left to deliberate about.

However, it is not just the abstract character of the public sphere, but also the *asymmetrical structure* of mass communication that turns participants in deliberation, who must face questions and objections, into more or less passive spectators and consumers.[31] Whereas deliberation requires reciprocity in assuming the roles of speaker and addressee, mass communication in the public sphere is best understood by analogy with a stage which does not permit an exchange of roles between the few actors and an anonymous watching public. To be sure, the actors perform for the public; but the latter can only offer blanket applause or express their disapproval at the end of an act or of the performance – they can't talk back. This 'asymmetrical' structure is embodied in two types of actor who play a constitutive role in the dramaturgy of the public sphere: the media experts, in particular the journalists, who produce news bulletins, commentaries, and reports; and the politicians, who occupy the centre of the political system and feature both as co-authors and as addressees of public opinions.

Without these actors, a public sphere would not be possible in national societies. They do not engage in deliberations among themselves, for example, but try to shape the opinions of an anonymous public without having to expose themselves to critical questioning.[32] Journalists have no need to do so because they work for the media – in other words, they exercise a specialized profession in which they expose themselves to public criticism only in the exceptional case of professional misconduct. As a highly professional politics becomes mediatized, politicians can adopt an increasingly populist relation to their potential voters, one geared to electoral success.

Internet communication on the World Wide Web seems to counterbalance the weaknesses associated with the anonymous and asymmetrical character of mass communication because it makes it possible to reintegrate interactive and deliberative elements into an unregulated exchange between partners who communicate with one another as equals, if only virtually. As it happens, the Internet has not only given rise to inquisitive surfers but has also revived the historically submerged phenomenon of an egalitarian public of reading and writing conversational partners and correspondents. On the other hand, computer-based communication can claim unequivocal democratic merits only for a specific context: it undermines censorship by authoritarian regimes which try to control and suppress spontaneous public opinions.

A different trend is prevalent under liberal regimes, however. Here the emergence of millions of 'chat rooms' scattered throughout the world and of globally networked 'issue publics' tends rather to fragment the huge mass public, which in the public sphere is centered on the same issues at the same time in spite of its size. This public disintegrates in virtual space into a large number of contingent fragmented groups, held together by special interests. As a result, the existing national publics seem to be undermined rather than reinforced. The Web provides the hardware for the delocalization of an intensified and accelerated mode of communication, but it can itself do nothing to stem the centrifugal tendencies. For the present, there are no functional equivalents, in this virtual space, for the structures of publicity which reassemble the decentralized messages, sift them, and synthesize them in edited form. Political communication within national publics seems at present to be able to benefit from online debates only when groups which are active on the Web refer to real processes, such as election campaigns or current controversies, for example, in an attempt to mobilize the interest and support of members.[33] An example of this anchoring of computer-based communication in processes taking place outside the virtual world is that of the groups of supporters of political parties, or that of the news groups which crystallize around particular newspapers and journals and their articles.[34]

Appealing to the Internet cannot dispel the *prima facie* doubt over the potentially positive contribution of mass communication to deliberative politics. We must instead examine the assumption which informs this pessimistic diagnosis. For it is by no means a foregone conclusion that media-based mass communication needs to resemble the demanding communicative design of discourses if it is to promote deliberative politics.

IV The Structure of Mass Communication and the Formation of Considered Public Opinions

In what follows I will try to explain why neither the abstract character of a public sphere dominated by the

158

mass media nor the asymmetrical relation which mass communication produces between the actors and their public needs to count against the applicability of the model of deliberative politics.

(1)   In national societies, the cycle of political communication circulates between *three levels*. I distinguish between

- the level of 'institutionalized discourse' at the centre of the political system, where the binding decisions concerning political programs and their implementation are prepared; and both
- the level of 'media-based mass communication' with a more or less passive public of readers, listeners, and viewers, where public opinions take shape; and
- the level of 'everyday communication in civil society' among face-to-face interlocutors (or virtual addressees) in 'arranged' or informal publics, in which the latent attitudes of potential voters take shape over long periods of time.

At each of these levels, political communication assumes a different form in the respective arenas. The public sphere forms the loosely structured periphery to the densely populated institutional centre of the state, and it is rooted in turn in the still more fleeting communicative networks of civil society. The public sphere, which functions differently from the other two sectors, contributes to legitimation by producing political communication, by keeping it active, by steering – and *filtering* – it. Thus I understand the public sphere as an intermediate system of mass communication, situated between the formally organized deliberations and negotiations at the centre and the arranged or informal conversations which take place in civil society at the periphery of the political system.

   There is empirical evidence both for the rationalizing effect of discourses on decision-making processes in national legislatures[35] and courts, and for the learning effects of everyday political conversations among citizens.[36] Here I will limit my remarks to the potential contribution of the public sphere to a legitimation process which, taken as a whole, should satisfy the conditions of deliberative politics. The interplay between functionally specialized arenas at different levels of the political system also explains why issues and inputs in different contexts entail different burdens of proof and call for different degrees of publicity[37] and different styles of argument (negotiation versus discourse).[38] Only across the full scope of the process of legitimation can 'deliberation' perform the filtering function which justifies the supposition that the process of political will formation fishes the reasonable elements of opinion formation out of the murky streams of political communication.

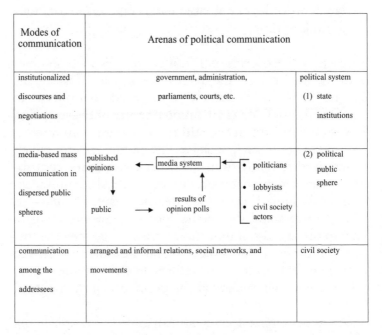

Figure 9.1   Arenas of Political Communication

The state, comprising the familiar complex of institutions – parliaments, courts, executive and administrative bodies, coalition panels, committees, and so on – forms the core of the political system. The corresponding end products – laws and political programs, judicial findings, official guidelines and policies, regulations and measures – are the result of institutionalized deliberation and decision-making processes. At the periphery of the system, the public sphere is embodied in the networks of communication conducted through the mass media. The public sphere acquires political relevance in the first instance as a domain of *published* opinions, which are selected by the media for broadcast from among the contributions of various actors. The primary sources of the contents are politicians and political parties, lobbyists and 'pressure groups', and also experts and actors in civil society. We can distinguish the spectrum of published opinions from the spectrum of opinions elicited by questioning – that is, the results of opinion polls. The latter reflect the statistically recorded attitudes of the population as they develop within the 'weak', dispersed public of the mass media. These attitudes are also shaped by public meetings and episodic encounters within civil society, and they generally fluctuate only within the limits of the political culture in question.

Media-based communication consists mainly in a discourse initiated and conducted by elites. In addition to the most important players – media professionals and professional politicians – Bernhard Peters distinguishes the following groups of actors, who feature on the virtual stage of a public sphere dominated by the mass media:[39] *lobbyists*, who represent the organized interests of the social subsystems; *advocates* of general interests, who represent the corresponding organizations (for instance Doctors without Borders) or who ensure that the voices of marginalized and under-represented groups first gain a public hearing; *experts*, whose advice is sought on the basis of their professional or scientific expertise; *moral entrepreneurs*, who draw public attention to neglected issues; and *intellectuals* who have acquired a certain reputation in their profession (for instance as authors or researchers), who (in contrast to lobbyists and experts) become involved without being solicited, with the aim of promoting ostensibly general interests.

(2)   In order to be able to judge whether a public sphere thus constituted can make a reasonable contribution to the process of legitimation, we must ascertain what contribution it is supposed to make from a normative point of view. According to the deliberative model, deliberation – as an essential component of the democratic procedure – is supposed to support the supposition

- that relevant issues and controversial answers, requisite information and appropriate arguments for and against will be mobilized;
- that the alternatives which emerge will be subjected to examination in argumentation and will be evaluated accordingly; and
- that rationally motivated 'yes' and 'no' positions on procedurally correct decisions will be the deciding factor.

Taking the legitimation process as a whole, it is the role of the public sphere to perform the first of these functions. The elites which take part in public communication are expected on the one hand to absorb impulses from civil society and to send them back, in a reworked form, to the public of voters, and on the other hand to place relevant issues and suitable inputs onto the agendas of the political bodies and to observe and comment upon the institutionalized deliberation and decision-making processes themselves. *Reflected public opinions* – as products of the public sphere itself – are supposed to result from this communicative circuit running between the centre and the periphery.

   This is still a pretty demanding expectation. Specifying necessary conditions for the production of relevant and sufficiently reflexive public opinions is nevertheless useful in so far as it endows the research on communication with standards for identifying and analysing the causes of pathologies in communication. I would like to develop such a normatively rich yet empirically applicable model in two steps, beginning with an examination of the interaction between the state and civil society on the one side, and the ensemble of functional systems on the other.

The democratic state finds itself confronted with demands from both sides. In addition to rules and regulations, the state has to provide public goods and services for its citizens as well as subsidies and public infrastructure for various functional subsystems, such as industry and the labor market, health care, traffic, energy, research and development, education, etc. Through lobbies, public relations, and neo-corporatist negotiations, representatives of the functional subsystems confront the administration with what they present as 'functional imperatives'. Pressure groups can employ the threat of the 'malfunction' of a particular system, for instance redundancies, capital flight, or growth in inflation, a breakdown in traffic, energy shortages, a shortfall of skilled workers, a brain drain, and so on. On the other hand, it is the citizens in their role as clients of the corresponding functional subsystems who experience such crises as lifeworld stress. Functional breakdowns are translated through class structures and stratification into unequal social impositions. Committed citizen groups, advocates, churches, and intellectuals within civil society can interpret the perceived social problems in the light of competing requirements of justice, and they can make corresponding political demands. The deficiencies which various social groups experience in their lifeworlds find expression in the public sphere through civil society, and these public opinions in turn shape the attitudes of potential voters, who exploit the competition between political parties and are in a position to threaten the government with a withdrawal of legitimation.

(3)   However, votes do not grow 'naturally' out of the soil of civil society. Election campaigns have a comparatively minor influence on longer-term opinions and attitudes. The latter develop continuously, acquire stability, and change only very gradually, both in the episodic publics of everyday communication and in the weak public of the inattentive addressees of the mass media. Only events which are perceived as dramatic or social movements can trigger drastic shifts in opinions. Because the political system depends on democratic legitimation, it presents an exposed flank to civil society in the shape of the public sphere which is instrumental in affirming and restructuring relations of political power through the informal pressure exercised by public opinions and through the formal mechanism of general elections. The centre and the periphery of the political system differ in their respective levels of density of institutions. Whereas the legally binding force of 'political power' is attached to offices, the 'political influence' of public opinions grows out of a network of criss-crossing flows of communication. The political institutions and offices authorize their holders to make collectively binding decisions in accordance with democratic procedures based on representation and delegation. By contrast, the basic rights to freedom of opinion and to freedom of the press, together with the constitution of the media [*Medienverfassung*] – that is, the legal guarantees of the diversity and independence of the mass media – constitute a framework which *makes possible* the emergence of influential public opinions out of the unbridled dynamism of 'wild' circuits of communication.

The networks of media and of news agencies form the infrastructure of the public sphere. Organizations for public opinion research continuously observe and record the attitudes of passive and anonymous mass publics. Media professionals produce an elite discourse which is fuelled by the contributions of various actors. These actors, who compete for access to the broadcast media and who wish to exercise as much influence as possible on the content of the programs, enter the forum of the public sphere from three angles, as it were: politicians and political parties come from the centre of the political system; lobbyists and special interest groups represent functional systems; and advocates, public interest groups, churches, intellectuals, and nongovernmental organizations have their roots in civil society.

Along with the journalists, all of these actors are involved in the production of *public opinions*. By the latter I understand clusters of controversial issues and inputs to which the parties concerned intuitively attach *weights* in accordance with their perceptions of the cumulative 'yes' and 'no' stances of the wider public. Public opinions exert influence. They form a milieu to which thoughts and feelings adjust, and thereby they exercise an indirect pressure on opinions and attitudes; in the long run, they influence the formation of mentalities. The influence of 'the' public opinion (in other words, the predominant opinion among the several public opinions) branches out, on the one side in the direction of a carefully observing government, and on the other in the direction of the mass public from which it originated and which now becomes reflexively aware of the opinions which acquired supremacy within its midst. Public opinions are hard to pin down empirically. In the final analysis they are the result of an intuitive bridging of the perceived differences between the *published* opinions, which are strongly shaped by the quality press on the one hand and by the representative spectrum of polled opinions reflected in survey data on the other. Thus they are the imponderable outcomes of the efforts of opinion-forming elites and of the more or less conscious reactions of a broad and diverse mass audience.

165

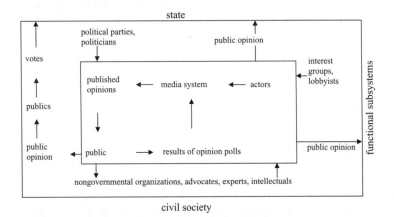

Figure 9.2 Public Sphere: Inputs and Outputs

The fact that both the administration and the voting public can adopt an affirmative, neutral, or negative position *again* on what imposes itself as 'public opinion' is an indication of the peculiarly reflexive character of the public sphere. People can take *an additional* stance on what they perceive as public opinion. Such reflexive responses 'from above', from the political system, and 'from below', from civil society, constitute a double test of how effectively political communication functioning as a filtering mechanism. For this reason, the abstract and asymmetrical structure of mass communication is not per se an obstacle to the formation of 'considered public opinions'. By this term I understand a pair of contrary, more or less coherent opinions, weighted in accordance with agreement and disagreement, which refer to a relevant issue and express what appears at the time, in the light of available information, to be the most plausible or reasoned interpretations of a sufficiently relevant – though generally controversial – issue.

From the viewpoint of political elites, such considered opinions fix the parameters for the range of possible decisions which the public of voters would accept as legitimate. At the same time they provide points of orientation for voters who can decide between competing platforms and programs. In the end, it is the aggregate of the votes actually cast by individual voters on election day that establishes the formal connection between the political communication at the periphery and the division of power at the centre of the political system: 'In competitive democracies the relevance of public opinion for both the public and the decision-makers ... is ultimately assured through the electoral procedure.'[40]

Notwithstanding the abstract and asymmetrical structure of mass communication, the media-dominated public sphere in geographically extensive national societies can generate considered public opinions *under favorable conditions*, and thus it can contribute to the deliberative quality of the political process in the way envisaged for this sector by the deliberative model. The conditional formulation recalls the second of the reservations alluded to above. The influence of *illegitimate* power-holders on the public sphere can, of course, distort the dynamics of mass communication to such an extent that the latter would no longer be able to satisfy the normative expectation, and thus would cease to operate in such a way that the relevant topics, requisite information, and appropriate arguments would find expression in each case and would succeed in crossing the threshold of the institutionalized processes of deliberation and decision-making.

V The Power Structures of the Public Sphere and the Dynamics of Mass Communication

Power is not per se illegitimate from a normative point of view. For our purposes, it is sufficient to distinguish four categories of power. *Political power* inherently requires legitimation, hence a justification which is accepted for whatever reason, at least passively, by those subjected to it. The acquisition and exercise of political power in the constitutional state calls for a demanding form of legitimation, namely the *reasonable* agreement of all citizens to the principles and procedures of the political decision-making process. The fact that such a regime is worthy of being recognized is justified by the connection between the inclusion of all citizens in the political formation of opinions and desires and the reasonable structure – thus a sufficient assurance of the deliberative quality – of this same process. *Social power* rests on status within a stratified society and is generally attached to positions within functional systems. *Economic power* is a special form of social power – the dominant form in capitalist societies. In a constitutional state, social power as such is not in the need of legitimation; however, the *conversion* of social power into influence over political decision-making must occur in a transparent manner. Attempts to exercise political influence must not bypass the normal public channels. The actors who emerge from civil society satisfy this requirement as a matter of course when their influence rests on their standing in the public sphere alone. Apart from their organizational power over their own members, these actors do not possess 'power' in the strict sense. Their public influence is based instead on the 'social' or 'cultural' capital they have accumulated in the form of social connections, media visibility, renown, reputation, or 'moral status' (as in the case of churches, for example). Since the mass media constitute another source of power, media professionals enjoy a special category of power.[41] This *media power* is based on the technology and infrastructure of mass communication. Those who work in the politically relevant sectors of the media system – reporters, columnists, editors, publishers, directors, and producers – cannot fail to exercise power inasmuch as they select and process politically relevant material and thus influence the formation of public opinions. Even if the press or the electronic media merely produced news and conveyed information, they would operate like filters; for they can let pass only a tiny proportion of the potential messages – just a few drops from of the massive flood of information, as it were. But contents are not just selected;

they also have to be presented and stylized in one format or another. The style and format of a presentation play a role in determining 'the quota' – the number of addressees reached and the level of attention generated. Media power consists in general in the ability to decide about the choice of content of a program and about its format – in other words the perspective from which an issue is presented or 'framed'. Media power can be measured by the resonance which a program generates in the public sphere, for example in terms of influencing the contents, priorities, and time frame of an agenda.[42] Journalists can wield power through agenda setting and issue framing, for in this way they intervene in the distribution of public influence among actors who compete for 'more influence' in the public sphere.

Despite this, democratic theory regards media power as harmless, as long as journalists operate within the guidelines of the public task of a 'free' press and of an 'independent' media system, as laid down by the constitution. A necessary condition for this 'presumption of innocence' is the editorial independence of the media from pressure exercised by politically, economically, and socially powerful actors. This is a relatively recent development even in western societies, and it does not reach back much further than the end of the Second World War.[43] For the media system, functional independence means self-regulation in accordance with a professional code, which finds expression both formally, in more or less exacting laws regulating the media (these guarantee at least diversity of opinion), and informally, in the professional ethics of industry-specific associations, self-administering bodies, and so on.[44]

The print and electronic media draw their politically relevant material from both inside and outside the media system. Television is now the primary source of political news in western societies,[45] and this popular medium is more widely disseminated than the so-called prestige media. But there is an informal hierarchy, which accords the national quality press – that is, the national daily and weekly newspapers and the weekly political magazines – the role of opinion leaders in inter-media agenda setting. Political news and commentaries from the leading newspapers and magazines with nationwide circulation function both as models and as stimuli for the other media.[46]

As far as external inputs are concerned, politicians and political parties are, of course, by far the most important suppliers. They produce and supply the lion's share of political events, news, and commentaries. They are in a strong position to negotiate privileged access to the media. However, even governments do not generally have any control over how the media convey and interpret their messages, or even over how the political elites or the broader public receive and react to them.[47] A further group enjoying privileged access to the media is that of the representatives and spokespersons of functional systems. Due to their higher level of organization and greater material resources, lobbies and special interest groups are able to employ professional techniques of public relations and political marketing to transform their social power into public influence. The organizations, groups, and activists which are supposed to represent general interests can also employ the methods of corporate communication management in certain instances. Examples are the spectacular actions of Amnesty International. But civil society actors are in a weaker position by comparison with politicians and lobbyists. Aside from temporary gains in publicity, they can make up for their lack of funding and of professionalism only during periods of political mobilization, when they benefit from social movements or can take advantage of the resonance of a restive periphery.

The players who feature on the virtual stage of the public sphere form a hierarchy, depending on which category of power or 'capital' they have at their disposal. Favorable opportunities to transform power into public influence through the channels of mass communication are not equally distributed. Some types of actors regularly enjoy better opportunities to intervene than others. Of course, this stratification reflects an imbalance in power, though the power in question is limited by the peculiar reflexivity of the public sphere. By this is meant that all of the parties involved can take *an additional* stance on, and react to, what they perceive as 'public opinion'. It is the joint construction of 'the' public opinion that invites actors to attempt to intervene strategically in the public sphere in the first place. All actors, whether they come from the centre of the political system, from the ensemble of functional systems or from civil society, intervene with *the same* intention of engaging in the shaping and reshaping of public opinion. The professional means of communication management are certainly expensive, and not everybody can afford them. Yet an unequal distribution of the means of effective influence does not necessarily prevent the formation of considered public opinions. The qualification 'not necessarily' reminds us of important conditions that must be met. For strategic interventions in the formation of public opinion run the risk of becoming inefficient unless play by the rules of the game. They must contribute to the mobilization of important issues, concrete facts, and convincing arguments, *which are in turn exposed to critical examination.*

However, powerful actors find themselves compelled to play by these rules only if the *established* rules are the correct ones, hence the kind of rules which guarantee that the game is geared to the production of considered public opinions. Yet such opinions can emerge only from the right kind of feedback between a self-regulated dynamics of media-based political communication and reasonable inputs from a responsive civil society. Two conditions must be fulfilled for such a game to come about: as we have seen, a self-regulating media system must acquire sufficient independence from its social environments; at the same time, however, civil society must also enable its citizens to participate in an inclusive process of public opinion formation. This invites the question of whether we can reasonably expect the consumers of mass media to exhibit the necessary dispositions and capabilities for participating autonomously in political communication.

The addressees who comprise the dispersed mass audience can play their part in a process of deliberative legitimation only if they manage to grasp the main lines of a, let us assume, more or less reasonable elite discourse and adopt more or less considered stances on relevant public issues. This is, at least at first sight, a startlingly excessive requirement. For the literature on 'public ignorance' paints a rather sobering picture of the average citizen as largely uninformed and uninterested.[48] The attention of potential readers and television and radio audiences to public issues is a scarce resource, and certainly the one which is most fiercely contested in the public arena. Besides, the corresponding motivational dispositions and the requisite cognitive abilities for storing and processing political messages are unevenly distributed among the population. Both factors speak for a high degree of selectivity and a high level of inattentiveness in the reception of political programs.

More recent studies on the cognitive role of information shortcuts in the long-term development and consolidation of political orientations, however, have led to a correction of this rather pessimistic picture. Quite apart from the question of whether the empirical studies conceptualize something like the political ignorance of citizens correctly at all,[49] the disappointing results do not directly support the unequivocal inferences often drawn from them. Readers, listeners, and viewers develop reasonable opinions on political issues in the long run, albeit through more or less unconscious processes. The relevant attitudes take shape through an accumulation of often tacit and later forgotten reactions to casually absorbed bits and pieces of information, which are initially assessed against the background of evolving conceptual schemes: 'thus people can be knowledgeable in their reasoning about their political choices without possessing a large body of knowledge about politics'.[50]

I would like to pause here to consider a provisional conclusion. Should we say that there are no prima facie reasons for the assumption that political communication in our so-called media society is at odds with the normative requirements of deliberative politics? The purpose of the present essay is to examine the empirical content and applicability of the deliberative model of democracy. I first mentioned some empirical evidence which supports the background assumption that deliberation can develop a truth-tracking potential in those communicative settings which we encounter within suitably designed political institutions at the top, and in everyday talk at the bottom, of the political system. The structure of mass communication coheres with the design of a deliberative legitimation process as well. But the interventions of powerful actors in the public sphere leave the formation of considered public opinions intact only under two rather demanding conditions. First, a self-regulating media system must maintain its independence vis-à-vis its environments, while connecting political communication in the public sphere with both civil society and the political centre. And, second, an inclusive civil society must empower citizens to participate in, and to respond to, a public discourse which, in turn, must not degenerate into a colonizing mode of communication.

VI Pathologies of Political Communication in the Light of the Deliberative Model

The foregoing rough reflections were intended to show that the way political communication is legally institutionalized in our kind of media society and the way it functions need not *necessarily* contradict the normative expectations of the deliberative model. Granted, appearances already reveal the discrepancy between these expectations and the actual relations. For this reason I

173

propose to clarify the *critical meaning* of a research design which is sufficiently realistic, even though it is informed by substantive norms. The deliberative model enables us to specify the conditions under which the public sphere *would* make an appropriate contribution to the process of legitimation: above all, the relative independence of the self-steering media system (1) and the right kind of feedback between civil society and media-based communication (2).[51] Conflicting data acquire a different, not merely destructive meaning when they can be interpreted as critical indicators of deficiencies in the process of legitimation which are open to practical rectification. Viewed in this light, the two postulated conditions take on the heuristic role of directing our attention to the reasons for the existing gaps in legitimation.

(1) As regards the independence of the media system, we must distinguish between the historical phenomenon of an *incomplete* functional differentiation of the media system from its environments on the one side, and, on the other, the *de*differentiation of a media system which had already achieved a differentiated form (that is, a temporary interference with the independence of an already self-regulating media system). The state monopoly of the broadcasting system in post-war Italy provides an example of a symbiotic amalgamation with the political system. During the period when a change of government from the ruling Christian Democrats to the Communist opposition was blocked, each of the three major parties enjoyed the privilege of recruiting the personnel of one of the public television channels from its own ranks. This pattern ensured a certain degree of pluralism, but not professional independence in planning programs. The incomplete differentiation of mass communication from the core of the political system was responsible for a certain paternalistic tendency towards educating politically immature citizens, against which Berlusconi could all the more successfully react with his policy of market liberalism.[52]

174

Compared to a lack of differentiation, temporary dedif-
ferentiation seems to be the lesser evil. Nevertheless, this
variant can have even graver consequences. A recent case
in point is the manipulation of the American public
through the amazingly successful communication policy
of the White House before and after the March 2003
invasion of Iraq by American troops. What sets this case
apart from similar successful campaigns is not so much
the clever and effective gambit of the President, who was
bent on going to war, in interpreting the terrorist attack
of 11 September 2001 as immediately triggering a 'war
against terrorism'. The positive echo which this uncon-
vincing definition met with can be easily explained in
sociopsychological terms.[53] In view of the shock caused
by that horrendous and heinous terrorist attack among the
American population, the interpretation seemed to fit the
event all too well. The remarkable thing was the absence
of competing attempts to place the monstrous event in a
different context, or to 'frame' it differently. Compared
to the parallel reports and commentaries in the European
press, the American print media, especially quality newspapers like the *New York Times*, failed to offer competing
interpretations as a timely corrective to the dangerously
misleading information policy of the government.[54] The
case of Judith Miller – a well-known journalist who
allowed herself to become a mouthpiece of government
propaganda in exchange for privileged access to the sources
of power – sheds light in hindsight on the spectacular
marketing of the war by the White House. Judged
by liberal standards, a responsible press should have provided the broader public with more reliable information
and more pertinent interpretations, through an inter-
media exchange with the popular press and television
stations.

A different case is the media's lack of distance from
associations and organizations representing economic
or other special interests. This is a less spectacular but
much more frequent occurrence than the temporary

entanglement of the press and television in the clutches of the government. Whether lobbies succeed in winning the attention of broader sectors of the population for their special concerns and for a favorable interpretation of these concerns also depends, of course, on organizational power and on material resources, in particular on advertising budgets. Apart from surreptitious advertising and corruption, however, favorable media coverage cannot simply be 'bought'. Only when specific policies, such as gun control or the regulation of the sale of pharmaceuticals, affect essential interest of large corporations or important economic sectors do concerted efforts to translate economic power into political influence through public relations campaigns achieve measurable effects. The indirect influence of scientific communities should also be mentioned in this context. The influence of the neoliberal doctrines of the Chicago School on the so-called 'Washington Consensus' even had worldwide repercussions.

A special case is the damage which the editorial independence of the media always suffers when private owners of media empires develop political ambitions which go beyond their proper, economic function and use their economic power in order to acquire political influence. Private newspapers and broadcasting companies are economic enterprises just like any others. But their owners can use their economic power to convert media power *directly* into public influence. Rupert Murdoch is the prime contemporary example of such a tycoon. He threw the weight of his newspapers and networks behind the ambitions of politicians like Margaret Thatcher, George W. Bush, and Tony Blair. A less typical example is provided by another media mogul, Silvio Berlusconi, who benefited from an unusual constellation. First he exploited the legal opportunities of media ownership for political self-promotion, and then, after the takeover of government, he influenced legislation in order to consolidate both his political success and his private fortune. In the course of this adventure, he even succeeded in changing

176

the whole media culture of his country, which until then had been marked by a degree of political tutelage by the parties, into a populist marketing of unpolitical entertainment – 'a mixture of films and telefilms, quiz and variety shows, cartoons and sports, with football pre-eminent in this latter category'.[55]

(2)   The second condition concerns the feedback between a self-steering media system and a civil society equipped with its own, more or less autonomous, publics which is responsive to communicative impulses. For democratic legitimation depends essentially on the right kind of inputs into the political system, namely ones which reflect the full spectrum of interests of the population. From a normative point of view, citizen participation must not exhaust itself in influencing the composition of parliamentary bodies and of the government through the results of general elections. Apart from the fact that the attitudes of the voters are also formed within the milieu of public opinions, collectively binding political decisions should always be taken under the scrutiny of a commenting and monitoring public. On the other hand, the involvement of civil society is possible only if the media-based communication has an impact on citizens who are willing and able to participate in the formation of considered public opinions by taking stances on controversial social issues. Two principal causes are cited to explain the systematic lack of this kind of feedback. On the one hand, social deprivation and cultural marginalization explain a selective access to, and uneven participation in, media-based political communication (a); at the same time, the colonization of the public sphere by market imperatives seems to foster a peculiar kind of paralysis among the consumers of mass communication (b).

(2a)   It is common knowledge in sociology that the interest in public affairs and the consumption of political news media are strongly correlated with cultural background

and social status (occupation and level of income, education, religious affiliation, and the like).[56] These data
can be interpreted as rough indicators of an insufficient
functional differentiation of the public sphere from the
mentality-shaping social milieus in which civil society
potentials are formed.[57] In the post-war period, however,
ascriptive ties between political behavior and social and
cultural backgrounds have progressively loosened. Long-
term studies on variations in interests in different political
dimensions – activities, value-orientations, party and
voting preferences – point to an increasing independence
of political attitudes from determinants such as place of
residence, social class, or religious affiliation.[58] These
changes go hand-in-hand with the well-known trend from
materialist to postmaterial values, and also with the
increasing importance of short-term ('fashion-dependent')
attitudes towards current affairs and topical issues. The
shift from voting behavior marked by long-term partisan-
ship and allegiances to particular political parties to issue
voting reveals, among other things, the growing impact of
public discourse on voter behavior. In addition, the trend
towards the formation of so-called 'issue publics', that is,
of groups which come together around shared interests in
specific issues, could be a pointer towards the increasing
importance of public, or at any rate media-transmitted,
impulses. Since ever more people have an interest in an
increasing number of different issues, a pluralism of such
issue-centered groups is emerging. However, this trend
has effects only in so far as the issue publics enter into
overlapping networks which counteract the fragmentation
of the voting public.[59]

   In spite of the inclusion of ever more citizens in the
flows of mass communication, the relevant studies arrive
at a very cautious assessment of the scope and depth of
media effects ('not so minimal'); and the conclusions
concerning the nature of the influence of mass communication on the involvement of citizens in politics are at best
ambivalent, if not downright pessimistic.[60] Certain find-

ings for the United States support the 'video malaise' hypothesis, which holds that people who make more extensive use of electronic media and consider them an important source of information have a lower level of trust in, and are more likely to take a cynical attitude towards, politics.[61] However, in so far as the consumption of television and radio programs even fosters feelings of powerlessness, apathy, and indifference towards politics, we must look for the causes in the formats and contents of political communication, and not in a general paralysis of civil society.

(2b)   The worldwide success of neoliberal policies, which advocate the substitution of self-regulating markets for political regulation, tends to reinforce the impression that the displacement of domains of political regulation by self-regulating markets is restricting the scope of action of national governments. The perception that political elites are increasingly helpless may also nourish feelings of powerlessness, apathy, and futility among the broader public of citizens. The aforementioned data suggest, however, that the mode of presentation and content of mass communication contribute to an alienation of the citizens from politics, and thus to the spread of privatism and of the mood of anti-politics.[62] This shift in the style of mass communication reveals a trend towards a redefinition of political questions in terms of the categories of advertising. The historical example of the emergence of an autonomous art and of an independent press during the eighteenth century shows that the reorientation of the production and distribution of cultural products to the conditions of market exchange can have a completely different, emancipatory effect. The marketing of cultural products does not lead inevitably to the commodification both of the content and of the reception of these goods. It is only when the functional imperatives of the market interfere with the 'internal logic' of the production and presentation of messages and programs in broadcasting that one mode of communication is surreptitiously replaced by another. *Infotainment* is one of the catchwords for the adjustment of political discussion to the style and substance of entertainment.

Marketing strategies no longer determine just the organization of election campaigns, but also the continuous media presence of leading politicians who try to establish direct and continuous contact with mass audiences which bypasses public discourse. The increasing importance of the 'image' of candidates for voting decisions explains the candidate-centered election strategies, which now extend across the whole period in office.[63] The above-mentioned trend towards election outcomes based on *single-issue* voting is being overlaid and surpassed by the latter trend, towards election decisions based on the *personal profile* of a candidate. The personalization of politics and the commodification of programs reinforce one another. Private radio and television stations whose budgets are based on extensive advertising are pioneers in this field. Although the publicly financed stations maintain a somewhat different program structure, public broadcasting is in the process of adapting to its private competitors.[64] Political programs are being cut back and trimmed to consumer friendliness. Further signs of the imperatives of 'consumer-friendliness' which are now beginning to affect news programs in Germany are, in addition to the personalization of serious debates, the dramatization of events, the crude simplification of complex matters, and a polarizing exaggeration of conflicts. The roles of citizen and consumer are beginning to merge. Some authors even think that political journalism in the traditional sense is an outdated model.[65]

These are just a few examples of how the deliberative research design can be put to critical use. Of course, such a use is possible only as long as the design itself is sufficiently anchored in empirical reality. My goal was to render this reference to empirical reality plausible. Public spheres are contingent on a whole range of presuppositions and, as such, they represent improbable evolutionary achievements of modern western societies. We cannot be sure that we will continue to enjoy them even in their countries of origin. However, the decline of this complex and delicate structure of communication would entail the disappearance of an essential social foundation of the exacting political self-understanding of modern societies, namely that of constitutional democracies as self-determining associations of free and equal citizens.

VII A Brief Postscript: Public Spheres beyond the Nation–State?

I have confined myself to the political role played by national public spheres in the liberal constitutional states of the West. Focusing on the example of western societies is justified on historical grounds if we take the deliberative model of democracy as our starting point. This does not prejudge the question of its transferability to other cultures and societies.[66] A completely different question is raised by the most recent phase of globalization, which began in the last quarter of the twentieth century and has transformed the basis of the legitimation of the classical nation–state.[67]

We are at present witnessing the emergence of a highly interdependent world society, whose functional systems effortlessly permeate national borders. The growing need for coordination and regulation is supposed to be met by an expanding network of international organizations. Here political decisions are being taken whose import for the populations of the nation–states involved, as regards their nature, invasiveness, and persistence, is so great that international treaties can no longer provide sufficient legitimation for such a form of 'governance beyond the nation–state'. At any rate, this basis of legitimation no longer meets the standards established in constitutional states.

Within the national framework, the public sphere makes possible a continuous monitoring of, and participation in, decision-making by the citizens by formulating and implementing policies (through political parties, general elections, nongovernmental organizations, citizen initiatives, and social movements). By contrast, the citizens get wind of the political decisions negotiated by the delegates of national governments in nontransparent international organizations only after the fact, for example when ratification by parliament is required. Sometimes there is talk of a global public sphere. In fact, a temporary worldwide awareness of particular occurrences such as catastrophes or wars can arise. The Vietnam War was probably the first historical event which achieved global awareness in a strict sense. A kind of transient global public sphere crystallized around it via the channels of the respective national news reporting and commentary. But the perpetuation of transnational decision-making processes is not being offset by the emergence of continuous forms of monitoring and commentary of comparable scope. The international institutions do not satisfy the essential prerequisites of transparency, accessibility, and responsiveness either.[68]

The democratic deficit is especially drastic in the European Union. Without a European public sphere, even a sufficient extension of the competences of the European Parliament would fail to enable the citizens to monitor the ever-denser and ever more invasive political decisions of the European Commission and of the European Council of Ministers. Because no European public sphere exists, the citizens elect the European Parliament on the basis of the wrong issues – that is, national ones. At the same time, the legitimacy of the governments of the member states is being undermined because now they can only 'implement' the insufficiently legitimate decisions taken in Brussels. Since the public spheres within the national societies do not accord sufficient prominence to European issues, citizens cannot intervene in a timely manner in European decision-making processes. When these decisions finally trickle down to the national level, the political opinion and will formation of the citizens is no longer consulted.[69]

The 'absence of a European public sphere' is generally discussed under the misleading premise that the alternative is to erect a superstructure – namely to introduce a higher level of communication, with its own European-wide media operating in a second language. Although one (or a range of) shared second language(s) will become established in the European arena as a medium of everyday political and economic exchange, there is an elegant solution to the problem of the multilingual character of the European-wide media public sphere. The image of a multilayered cake is misleading. The solution does not consist in constructing a supranational public sphere, but in *transnationalizing* the existing national public spheres. For the latter could *become more responsive to one another* without any need for drastic changes in the existing infrastructure.[70] At the same time, the boundaries of the national public spheres would become portals for mutual translations. The existing quality newspapers could salvage their economically precarious existence by, among other things, assuming the role of transnational scouts in the long-overdue extension of the role of national public spheres. Their role would not merely be to provide exposure to European issues and to treat them accordingly, but also to provide information concerning the political positions and controversies which trigger the same issues in *the other* member states.[71]

Afterword: Lessons of the Financial Crisis

Herr Habermas, the international financial system has collapsed and a global economic crisis is looming. What do you find most worrying about this?

What worries me most is the scandalous social injustice that the most vulnerable social groups will have to bear the brunt of the socialized costs for the market failure. The mass of those who are, in any case, not among the winners of globalization now have to pick up the tab for the impacts of a predictable dysfunction of the financial system on the real economy. Unlike the shareholders, they will not pay in money values but in the hard currency of their daily existence. Viewed in global terms, this avenging fate is also afflicting the economically weakest countries. That's the political scandal. Yet pointing the finger at scapegoats strikes me as hypocritical. The speculators, too, were acting consistently within the established legal framework, according to the socially recognized logic of profit maximization. Politics turns itself into a laughing stock when it resorts to moralizing instead of relying upon the enforceable law of the democratic legislator. Politics, and not capitalism, is responsible for promoting the common good.

You recently lectured at Yale University. Which images of this crisis left the deepest impression?

184

A seemingly endless loop of melancholic Hopperian images of long rows of abandoned houses in Florida and elsewhere, with 'Foreclosure' signs on their front lawns flickered across the television screens. Then you saw buses arriving with curious prospective buyers from Europe and wealthy Latin Americans, followed by the real estate agent showing them the closets in the bedroom smashed in a fit of rage and despair. After my return I was struck by the sharp contrast between the agitated mood in the United States and the calm feeling of 'business as usual' here in Germany. In the US, the very real economic anxieties coincided with the hot end spurt of one of the most momentous election campaigns in recent memory. The crisis also instilled a more acute awareness of people's personal interests in broad sectors of the electorate. It forced them to make decisions which were, if not necessarily more reasonable, then at least more rational, at any rate by comparison with the previous presidential election, which was ideologically polarized by '9/11'. America will owe its first black president – if I may hazard a prediction on the eve of the election – and hence a major historical watershed in the history of its political culture, to this fortunate coincidence. Beyond this, however, the crisis could also be the harbinger of a changed political climate in Europe.

What do you have in mind?

Such tidal shifts change the parameters of public discussion and, in the process, the spectrum of political alternatives seen as possible. The Korean War marked the end of the New Deal, whereas Reagan and Thatcher and the waning of the Cold War marked the end of the era of social welfare programs. Today, with the end of the Bush era and the bursting of the last neoliberal rhetorical balloons, the Clinton and New Labour programs have run their course too. What is coming next? My hope is that the neoliberal agenda will no longer be accepted at face value but will be open to challenge. The whole program of subordinating the lifeworld to the imperatives of the market must be subjected to scrutiny.

According to the neoliberal slogan, the state is just one player in the economic field and should play as small a role as possible. Is this way of thinking now discredited?

That depends on what course the crisis takes, on the perceptual capacities of the political parties and on the issues which find their way onto the public agenda. In Germany, at any rate, things are still strangely calm. The agenda which recklessly prioritizes shareholder interests and is indifferent to increasing social inequality, to the emergence of an underclass, to child poverty, of a low wage sector, and so on has been discredited. With its mania for privatization, this agenda hollows out the core functions of the state, it sells the remnants of a deliberating public sphere to profit-maximizing financial investors, and it subordinates culture and education to the interests and moods of sponsors who are dependent on market cycles.

Are the consequences of the privatization mania becoming apparent in the financial crisis?

In the United States the crisis is exacerbating the already apparent material, moral, social, and cultural damage caused by a policy of deregulation pushed to an extreme by the Bush administration. The privatization of social security and health care, of public transport, of the energy supply, of the penal system, of military security services, of large sectors in school and university education, and the surrender of the cultural infrastructure of cities and communities to the commitment and generosity of private sponsors are part of a social design whose risks and consequences are difficult to reconcile with the egalitarian principles of a social and democratic constitutional state.

State agencies are not capable of conducting business in accordance with economic imperatives.

Yes, but certain vulnerable areas of life should not be exposed to the risks of stock market speculation, a requirement which is not consistent with switching investments intended to provide for old age and retirement benefits to shares. In democracies there are also some public goods, for example undistorted political communication, which cannot be tailored to the profit expectations of financial investors; the citizens' need for information cannot be met by the culture of easily digestible sound bites which flourishes in a media landscape dominated by commercial television.

Are we experiencing a 'legitimation crisis' of capitalism, to quote the title of a controversial book of yours?

Since 1989–90, it has become impossible to break out of the universe of capitalism; the only option is to civilize and tame the capitalist dynamics from within. Even during the post-war period, the Soviet Union was not a viable alternative for the majority of the Left in western Europe. This was why, in 1973, I wrote on legitimation problems 'in' capitalism. These problems have forced themselves onto the agenda once again, with greater or lesser urgency depending on the national context. A symptom of this is the demands for caps on managers' salaries and the abolition of 'golden parachutes', that is, of the outrageous compensation payments and bonuses.

But aren't such policies merely window dressing? There are elections coming up next year.

Yes, this is of course symbolic politics designed to divert attention away from the failures of the politicians and their economic consultants. They have been aware of the need for regulation on the financial markets for a long time. I just reread Helmut Schmidt's crystal-clear article 'Beaufsichtigt die neuen Großspekulanten' ['Regulate the New Mega-Speculators'] from February 2007 (*Die Zeit*, No 30). Everyone knew what was going on. In America and Great Britain, however, the political elites viewed the wild speculation as useful as long as things were going well. And Europe succumbed to the Washington Consensus. In this regard there was also a broad coalition of the willing, for which Mr Rumsfeld didn't need to drum up support.

The Washington Consensus was the notorious economic plan, proposed by the IMF and the World Bank in 1990, which was supposed to provide the template for economic reform, first in Latin America and then throughout half of the world. Its central promise was 'Trickle Down': let the rich become richer and affluence will trickle down to the poor.

Empirical evidence of the falsehood of this prognosis has been accumulating for many years. The effects of the increase in affluence are so asymmetrical, both at the national and at the global level, that the zones of poverty have grown before our very eyes.

Let's do a bit of reckoning with history [Vergangenheitsbewältigung]: How did it come to this? Did the end of the communist threat strip capitalism of its inhibitions?

The form of capitalism reined in by nation–states and by Keynesian economic policies – which, after all, conferred historically unprecedented levels of prosperity on the OECD countries – came to an end somewhat earlier, already with the abandonment of the system of fixed exchange rates and with the oil crisis. The economic theory of the Chicago School acquired practical influence already under Reagan and Thatcher. This merely continued under Clinton and New Labour – and during the period of our most recent hero, Gordon Brown, as British finance minister. However, the collapse of the Soviet Union led to a fatal triumphalism in the West. The feeling of being among the winners of world history is seductive. In this case it contributed to inflating a theory of economic policy into a worldview permeating all areas of life.

Neoliberalism is a form of life. All citizens are supposed to become entrepreneurs of their own labor power and to become customers . . .

. . . and competitors. The stronger, who win out in the free-for-all of the competitive society, can claim this success as their personal merit. It is deeply comical how managers – though not they alone – fall prey to the absurd elitist rhetoric of our talk shows, let themselves be celebrated in all seriousness as role models, and mentally position themselves above the rest of society. It's as if they could no longer appreciate the difference between functional elites and the ascriptive elites of estates in early modern societies. What is so admirable about the character and mentality of people in leading positions who do their job in a half-competent manner? Another alarm signal was the Bush Doctrine announced in Fall 2002, which laid the groundwork for the invasion of Iraq. The social Darwinist potential of market fundamentalism has since become apparent in foreign policy as well as in social policy.

But Bush wasn't alone. He was flanked by an impressive horde of influential intellectuals.

Many of whom have learned nothing in the meantime. In the case of leading neoconservative thinkers like Robert Kagan, the thinking in terms of predatory categories à la Carl Schmitt has become if anything more pronounced since the Iraq disaster. His recent commentary on the current regression of international politics into a nuclear armed and increasingly unrestrained power struggle is: 'The world has returned to normal.'

But, to repeat: What went wrong at the political level after 1989? Did capital become too powerful vis-à-vis politics?

It became clear to me during the 1990s that politics must build up its capacities for joint action at the supranational level if it is to catch up with the markets. There even seemed to be initial steps in this direction during the early part of the decade. George Bush the elder spoke in a programmatic way of a New World Order and seemed to want to make use of the long blocked – and ridiculed! – United Nations. At first there was a sharp increase in the number of humanitarian interventions enacted by the Security Council. The politically intended economic globalization should have been followed by a system of global political coordination and by a further legal codification of international relations. However, the initial ambivalent efforts lost momentum already under Clinton. The current crisis is again drawing attention to this deficiency. Since the beginning of the modern era, the market and politics have had to be repeatedly balanced off against each other in order to preserve the network of relations of solidarity among the members of political communities. A tension between capitalism and democracy always remains, because the market and politics rest on conflicting principles. The flood of decentralized individual choices unleashed within more complex networks also calls for regulations after the latest phase of globalization; this is contingent on a corresponding extension of political procedures through which interests are generalized.

What does this mean? You continue to support Kant's cosmopolitanism and you advocate Carl Friedrich von Weizsäcker's idea of a global domestic politics. That sounds simply illusory. How should we picture it? After all, you need only think of the current state of the United Nations.

I must admit that a reform of the core institutions of the United Nations from the ground up would not go far enough. To be sure, the Security Council, the secretariat, the tribunals, and the powers and procedures of these institutions in general must as a matter of urgency be made fit for a global implementation of human rights and for the effective prohibition on violence – which is in itself an immense task. However, even if the United Nations Charter could be developed into a kind of constitution for the international community, this framework would still lack a forum in which the militarized struggle of the major powers would be transformed into institutionalized negotiations concerning the problems of the global economy in need of regulation – including problems of climate and environmental policy, of the distribution of contested energy resources, of scarce supplies of drinking water, and so on. At this transnational level problems of distribution arise which cannot be dealt with in the same way as violations of human rights or infringements of international security – ultimately, as prosecutable offences – but have to be worked out through political negotiations.

But an institution responsible for this already exists, the G8.

That's an exclusive club in which some of these issues are discussed in a noncommittal way. As it happens, there is a revealing discrepancy between the overhyped expectations associated with these events and the meager results of the media spectacles, which remain without consequences. The illusory weight of expectation shows that the populations are very well aware – perhaps even more acutely aware than their own governments – of the unresolved problems of a future global domestic politics.

That sounds suspiciously like the dreams of a ghost-seer.

Just a few days ago, most people would have regarded what is happening today as unrealistic. The European and Asian governments are outdoing each other with

191

regulatory proposals to rectify deficiencies in the institu-tionalization of the financial markets. Even the SPD in the CDU are presenting proposals on accounting rules and capital adequacy ratios, on the personal liability of managers, on improved transparency and oversight of the stock market, and so on. Of course, a tax on stock market transactions, which would already go some way towards a global tax policy, is rarely mentioned. In any case, the new 'architecture of the financial system', announced with much fanfare, will not be easy to implement against US resistance. As to whether it would even go far enough, given the complexity of these markets and the worldwide interdependence of the most important functional systems ... International treaties, which is what the parties cur-rently have in mind, can be revoked at any time. They cannot provide the basis for a watertight regime.

Even if new powers were transferred to the International Monetary Fund, that would not amount to a global domestic politics.

I don't want to make predictions. Given the scale of the problems, the most we can do is to think about constructive proposals. The nation–states must come to see themselves increasingly as members of the inter-national community – even in their own interest. That is the most difficult task which needs to be tackled over the next couple of decades. When we speak of 'politics' with the international stage in mind, we often think of the actions of governments which have inherited the self-understanding of collective actors who make sovereign decisions. Today, however, this self-understanding of the state as a Leviathan, which developed from the seven-teenth century onwards in tandem with the European system of states, has already lost its continuity. The sub-stance and composition of what we used to call 'politics' in the international arena is changing from one day to the next.

192

But how does this cohere with the social Darwinism in international relations which, as you claim, has experienced a resurgence on the global stage since 9/11?

Perhaps we should take a step back and consider a somewhat larger context. Since the late eighteenth century, law has gradually permeated the *politically constituted* power of government and stripped it of the substantive character of mere 'force' in the domestic sphere. In its external relations, however, the state has preserved enough of this substance, in spite of the growth of intertwined international organizations and in spite of the increasingly binding power of international law. The concept of the 'political' shaped by the nation–state is nevertheless in a state of flux. Within the European Union, for example, the member states continue to enjoy their monopoly on legitimate force, while nevertheless implementing the laws enacted at the supranational level more or less without demur. This transformation of law and politics is also bound up with a capitalist dynamics which can be described as a periodic interplay between a functionally driven opening followed in each case by a socially integrative closure at a higher level.

Does this mean that the market breaks open society and the welfare state closes it up again?

The welfare state is a late and, as we are now learning, fragile accomplishment. Expanding markets and communications networks have always had an explosive force, with simultaneously individualizing and liberating consequences for individual citizens; but each of these breaches has been followed by a reorganization of the old relations of solidarity within a more comprehensive institutional framework. This process began during the early modern period as the ruling estates of the High Middle Ages were progressively parliamentarized, as in England, or mediatized by absolute monarchs, as in France, within the new territorial states. The process continued in the wake of

193

the constitutional revolutions of the eighteenth and nineteenth centuries and in the wake of the welfare state legislative programs of the twentieth century. This legal taming of the Leviathan and class antagonism within civil society was no small matter. For the same functional reasons, however, this successful constitution-alization of state and society points today – after a further phase of economic globalization – to the constitutionaliza-tion of international law and of the strife-torn world society.

What role does Europe play in your scenario?

Not the one it has in fact played in the crisis. It is not clear to me why the recent crisis management of the Euro-pean Union is being praised so highly. Gordon Brown was able to bring the American Finance Minister Paulsen to reinterpret the laboriously negotiated bailout with his memorable decision because he brought the most impor-tant players in the Eurozone on board, through the media-tion of the French president and against the initial resistance of Angela Merkel and of her minister of finance, Peer Steinbrück. You need only examine this negotiation process and its outcome more closely. For it was the three most powerful of the nation–states which are united in the EU who agreed, as sovereign actors, to coordinate their different measures – which happened to point in the same direction. In spite of the presence of Messrs Juncker and Barroso, the way this classical international agreement came about had almost nothing to do with a joint political will formation of the European Union. The *New York Times* duly registered, not without a hint of malice, the Europeans' inability to agree upon a joint eco-nomic policy.

How do you account for that?

The present course of the crisis is making manifest the flaw in the construction of the European Union: every country is responding with its own economic measures. Because the competences in the Union, simplifying somewhat, are divided in such a way that Brussels and the European Court of Justice implement the economic freedoms, whereas the resulting external costs are shunted off onto the member states, there is at present no joint will formation at the level of economic policy. The most prominent member states are even divided over the principles governing how much state and how much market is desirable in the first place. Moreover, each country is conducting its own foreign policy, Germany first and foremost. The Berlin Republic, for all its quiet diplomacy, is forgetting the lessons of history drawn by the old Federal Republic. The government is exploiting the extended room for maneuver in foreign policy it has gained since 1989–90 and is falling back into the familiar pattern of national power politics between states, even though the latter have long ago shrunk to the format of minor princedoms.

But what could these princedoms do? What would be the next step?

Are you asking me for my wish list? Under the present conditions I regard graduated integration or different speeds of unification as the only possible scenario for overcoming the current stagnation. Thus Sarkozy's proposal for an economic government of the Eurozone can serve as a starting point. This does not mean that we would have to accept the statist background assumptions and protectionist intentions of its sponsor. Procedures and political results are two different things. The 'closer cooperation' in the field of economic policy would have to be followed by 'closer cooperation' in foreign policy. And neither could be conducted any longer through backroom deals behind the backs of the populations.

You won't find support for that even in the SPD.

195

The SPD leadership is abandoning this idea to the Christian Democrat Jürgen Rüttgers, the 'labor leader' in the Rhine and Ruhr region. All across Europe, the social democratic parties have their backs to the wall because they are being forced to play zero-sum games with shrinking stakes. Why don't they grasp the opportunity to break out of their national cages and gain a new room for maneuver at the European level? In this way they could even set themselves apart from the regressive competition from the Left. Whatever 'Left' and 'Right' still mean today, only together could the Eurozone countries acquire sufficient weight in world politics to be able to exert a reasonable influence on the agenda of the global economy. The alternative is to act as Uncle Sam's poodle and to throw themselves at the mercy of a global situation which is as dangerous as it is chaotic.

Speaking of Uncle Sam – you must be deeply disappointed with the United States. For you the US was supposed to serve as the draft horse of the new world order.

Do we have any alternative except to bet on this draft horse? The United States will emerge weaker from the current twofold crisis. However, it remains for the present the liberal superpower, and it finds itself in a situation which encourages it to overhaul its neoconservative self-image as the paternalistic global benefactor. The worldwide export of its own form of life sprang from the false, centralized universalism of the old empires. By contrast, modernity rests upon the decentralized universalism of equal respect for everyone. It is in the interest of the United States not only to abandon its counterproductive stance towards the United Nations but to place itself at the head of the reform movement. Viewed historically, the confluence of four factors – superpower status, the oldest democracy in the world, the assumption of office of a, let's hope, liberal and visionary president, and a political culture which provides an impressive sounding board for normative impulses – represents an improbable constellation. Today America is deeply distraught by the failure of the unilateral adventure, the self-destruction of neoliberalism and the abuse of its exceptionalist consciousness. Why shouldn't this nation, as it has done so often in the past, pull itself together and, before it is too late, try to bind the competing major powers of today – the global powers of tomorrow – into an international order which no longer needs a superpower? Why shouldn't an American president – buoyed by a watershed election – who finds that his scope for action in the domestic arena is severely constrained, want to embrace this reasonable opportunity – this opportunity for reason – at least in foreign policy?

The so-called realists would dismiss your proposal with a jaded smile ...

I realize that many things speak against it. The new American president would have to overcome the resistance of the elites within his own party who are subservient to Wall Street; he would doubtlessly also have to be dissuaded from succumbing to the reflexes of a new protectionism. In addition, the United States would need the friendly support of a loyal yet self-confident ally in order to undertake such a radical change in direction. A West which is 'bipolar' in a creative sense will become possible, of course, only when the EU learns to speak with one voice in foreign policy and, indeed, to use its internationally accumulated capital of trust to act in a far-sighted manner itself. The 'Yes, but ...' is obvious. Yet in times of crisis we may have more need of a somewhat broader perspective than that offered by the mainstream and the petty maneuvering of politics as usual.

Interview conducted by Thomas Assheuer

Notes

Chapter 1 '... And to define America, her athletic Democracy': In Memory of Richard Rorty

1 R. Rorty (ed.), *The Linguistic Turn: Essays in Philosophical Method* (Chicago: University of Chicago Press, 1967).
2 Ludwig Wittgenstein, *Culture and Value*, ed. by G. H. von Wright, trans. by Peter Winch (Oxford: Blackwell, 1980).
3 R. Rorty, *Philosophy and Social Hope* (New York: Penguin Books, 1999), pp. 190f.
4 R. Rorty, 'The World Well Lost', *The Journal of Philosophy* 69/19 (1972): 649–55. This title is an allusion to the 1953 short story of the same name by Theodore Sturgeon.
5 R. Rorty, 'Philosophy and the Future', in H. J. Saatkamp, Jr (ed.), *Rorty and Pragmatism: The Philosopher Responds to its Critics* (Nashville: Vanderbilt University Press, 1995), p. 199.
6 Walt Whitman, 'To Foreign Lands', in *Leaves of Grass* (New York: Mitchell Kennerley, 1897), p. 11.
7 This is the title of Adorno's related critique of Husserl's epistemology: Theodor W. Adorno, *Against Epistemology: A Metacritique*, trans. by Willis Domingo (Cambridge, MA: MIT Press, 1982).
8 Rorty, *Philosophy and Social Hope* (above, n. 3), p. 59.
9 Rorty (ed.), *The Linguistic Turn* (above, n. 1), p. 36.

10 Eduardo Mendieta (ed.), *Take Care of Freedom and Truth Will Take Care of Itself: Interviews with Richard Rorty* (Stanford, CA: Stanford University Press, 2006), p. 79.
11 *Ibid.*, p. 79.
12 Robert Brandom (ed.), *Rorty and his Critics* (Malden, MA: Blackwell, 2001).
13 Rorty, *Achieving Our Country: Leftist Thought in Twentieth -Century America* (Cambridge: Harvard University Press, 1998).
14 *Ibid.*, p. 19.
15 Quoted from Mendieta (ed.), *Take Care of Freedom*, (above, n. 10) p. 101.

Chapter 2 How to Answer the Ethical Question: Derrida and Religion

1 Habermas, 'Begegnungen mit Gershom Scholem', in *Münchner Beiträge zur jüdischen Geschichte und Kultur,* Vol. 2, pp. 9–18.
2 Derrida, 'The Future of the Profession or the University without Condition (Thanks to the 'Humanities', What *Could Take Place* Tomorrow)', in Tom Cohen (ed.), *Jacques Derrida and the Humanities: A Critical Reader* (Cambridge: Cambridge University Press, 2001), pp. 24–57.
3 Ibid., p. 54.
4 Habermas, *The Philosophical Discourse of Modernity*, trans. by Frederick Lawrence (Cambridge, MA: MIT Press, 1987), pp. 182ff.
5 Gershom Scholem, 'Zehn unhistorische Sätze über Kabbala', in idem, *Judaica III* (Frankfurt am Main: Suhrkamp, 1973), p. 264.
6 John Rawls, *Political Liberalism* (New York: Columbia University Press, 1998).
7 Søren Kierkegaard, *Either/Or: A Fragment of Life*, ed. and trans. by Alastair Hannay (London: Penguin, 1992), p. 553.
8 Ibid., pp. 550–1.
9 See in particular the conclusion 'The Moral', in Kierkegaard, *Philosophical Fragments. Johannes Climacus*, ed. and

trans. by Howard V. Hong and Edna H. Hong (Princeton, NJ: Princeton University Press, 1992), p. 111.

10 On what follows, see Michael Theunissen, *Das Selbst auf dem Grund der Verzweiflung: Kierkegaards negativistische Methode* (Frankfurt am Main: Hain, 1991).

11 Søren Kierkegaard, *The Sickness unto Death*, ed. and trans. by Howard V. Hong and Edna H. Hong (Princeton, NJ: Princeton University Press, 1980), pp. 52–3.

12 Ibid., p. 14.

13 Ibid., pp. 13–14.

14 Kierkegaard, *Philosophical Fragments* (above, n. 9), p. 45.

15 Karl Jaspers, *The Great Philosophers*, Vol. 1, ed. by Hannah Arendt, trans. by Ralph Manheim (London: Hart-Davis, 1962).

16 Karl Jaspers, *Der philosophische Glaube angesichts der Offenbarung* (Munich: Piper, 1962), pp. 100f.: 'Here knowledge does not stand over against faith, but faith over against faith … Revealed faith and rational faith stand in a polar relation to each other, they are affected by each other and, although they do not understand each other completely, they do not cese to try to understand each other. What each individual within himself rejects for himself, he can nevertheless recognize within the other as the latter's faith'.

17 Max Horkheimer, 'Theism and Atheism', in idem, *Critique of Instrumental Reason: Lectures and Essays Since the End of World War II*, trans. by Matthew J. O'Connell et al. (New York: Continuum, 1974).

18 On my critique of Horkheimer, see 'To Seek to Salvage an Unconditional Meaning without God Is a Futile Undertaking: Reflections on a Remark of Max Horkheimer', in J. Habermas, *Justification and Application: Remarks on Discourse Ethics*, trans. by Ciaran Cronin (Cambridge, MA: MIT Press, 1993), pp. 133–46.

19 Theodor W. Adorno, *Minima Moralia: Reflections from Damaged Life*, trans. by E. F. N. Jephcott (London: New Left Books, 1974), p. 247.

20 Ibid.

21 Ibid.

22 P. J. Huntington, 'Heidegger's Reading of Kierkegaard Revisited', in Martin J. Matustik and Merold Westphal

(eds), *Kierkegaard in Post/Modernity* (Bloomington and Indianapolis: Indiana University Press, 1995), pp. 43–65.
23 Martin Heidegger, *Nietzsche*, Vol. 3 (Pfullingen: Neske, 1961), p. 325.
24 Derrida, *Of Spirit: Heidegger and the Question*, trans. by Geoffrey Bennington and Rachel Bowlby (Chicago: Chicago University Press, 1989), pp. 109–13.
25 Ibid., p. 113.
26 In J. Habermas, *The Divided West*, trans. by Ciaran Cronin (Cambridge: Polity, 2006), pp. 87–8 (translation amended).

Chapter 3   Ronald Dworkin – A Maverick among Legal Scholars

1 'Law as integrity asks judges to assume ... that the law is structured by a coherent set of principles about justice and fairness and due process, and it asks them to enforce these in fresh cases that come before them, so that each person's situation is fair and just according to the same standards. That style of adjudication respects the ambition integrity assumes, the ambition to be a community of principle.' Ronald Dworkin, *Law's Empire* (Cambridge, MA: Harvard University Press, 1986), p. 243.
2 In Stuart Hampshire, Thomas Scanlon, Bernard Williams, Thomas Nagel and Ronald Dworkin, *Public and Private Morality* (Cambridge: Cambridge University Press, 1978), pp. 113–43.
3 Ronald Dworkin, *Justice for Hedgehogs: Synopsis* (unpublished ms., 2000; forthcoming), p. 1: 'We each have an enduring and special responsibility for living well, for making something of value of our own lives, as a painter makes something valuable of his canvas' (quoted with permission from the author).
4 'Our various responsibilities and obligations to others flow from that personal responsibility for our own lives. Only in some special roles and circumstances – principally in politics – do these responsibilities to others include any requirement of impartiality between them and ourselves.' Dworkin, *Truth for Hedgehogs*

(above, n. 3), p. 11 (quoted with permission from the author).
5 Ronald Dworkin, *Is Democracy Possible Here?* Princeton: Princeton University Press, 2006.

Chapter 4   An Avantgardistic Instinct for Relevances: The Role of the Intellectual and the European Cause

1 Karl Renner, *The Institutions of Private Law and Their Social Functions*, ed. by O. Kahn-Freund, trans. by Agnes Schwarzschild (London: Routledge & Keegan Paul,1949). The book initially appeared under the pseudonym 'Josef Kramer'.
2 I draw upon Renner in *The Structural Transformation of the Public Sphere*, trans. by Thomas Burger and Frederick Lawrence (Cambridge, MA: MIT Press, 1991), p. 149.
3 Max Adler, *Das Rätsel der Gesellschaft: Zur erkenntniskritischen Grundlegung der Sozialwissenschaft*, reprint of the 1936 Vienna edition (Aalen: Scientia, 1975).
4 I discuss Adler in 'Reflections on the Linguistic Foundation of Sociology: Christian Gauss Lectures (Princeton University, February–March 1971)', in J. Habermas, *On the Pragmatics of Social Interaction*, trans. by Barbara Fultner (Cambridge: Polity, 2001), p. 173 n. 18 and p. 174 n. 5.
5 G. Verhofstadt, *The United States of Europe* (London: The Federal Trust for Education and Research, 2006).

Chapter 5   What is Meant by a 'Post-Secular Society'? A Discussion on Islam in Europe

1 Detlef Pollack, *Säkularisierung – Ein moderner Mythos?* (Tubingen: Mohr Siebeck, 2003).
2 Hans Joas, 'Gesellschaft, Staat und Religion', in idem (ed.), *Säkularisierung und die Weltreligionen* (Frankfurt am Main: Fischer, 2007), pp. 9–43.
3 Jeffrey K. Hadden, 'Towards Desacralizing Secularization Theory', *Social Force* 65 (1987): 587–611.

4   Joas, 'Gesellschaft, Staat und Religion' (above, n. 2).

5   Peter L. Berger, 'The Desecularization of the World: A Global Overview', in idem (ed.), *The Desecularization of the World: Resurgent Religion and World Politics* (Grand Rapids, Michigan: W. B. Eerdmans, 1999), pp. 1–18.

6   Joachim Gentz, 'Die religiöse Lage in Ostasien', in Joas (ed.), *Säkularisierung und die Weltreligionen* (above, n. 2), pp. 358–75.

7   See the contributions of Hans Gerhard Kippenberg and Heinrich von Stietencron in Joas (ed.), *Säkularisierung und die Weltreligionen* (above, n. 2), pp. 465–507 and pp. 194–223.

8   Pippa Norris and Ronald Inglehart, *Sacred and Secular: Religion and Politics Worldwide* (Cambridge: Cambridge University Press, 2004).

9   J. Casanova, *Public Religions in the Modern World* (Chicago: University of Chicago Press, 1994).

10 J. Habermas, 'Faith and Knowledge', in *The Future of Human Nature*, trans. by Hella Beister and William Rehg (Cambridge: Polity, 2003), pp. 101–15.

11 Thus Francis Schüssler Fiorenza, 'The Church as a Community of Interpretation', in Don S. Browning and F. Schüssler Fiorenza (eds), *Habermas, Modernity, and Public Theology* (New York: Crossroad, 1992), pp. 66–91.

12 Geert Mak, *Der Mord an Theo van Gogh: Geschichte einer moralischen Panik* (Frankfurt am Main: Suhrkamp, 2005).

13 Thierry Chervel and Anja Seeliger (eds), *Islam in Europa* (Frankfurt am Main: Suhrkamp, 2007). The essays in this volume are available in English at *signandsight.com*: 'The "Islam in Europe" debate': http://www.signand-sight.com/features/1167.html (accessed December 2008).

14 Margriet de Moor, 'Alarm Bells in Muslim Hearts', *signandsight.com*, 23 April 2007: http://www.signand-sight.com/features/1309.html (accessed December 2008).

15 For a history and a systematic analysis, see the comprehensive study by Rainer Forst, *Toleranz im Konflikt* (Frankfurt am Main: Suhrkamp, 2003).

16 J. Habermas, 'Religious Tolerance as Pacemaker for Cultural Rights', in idem, *Between Naturalism and Religion*,

trans. by Ciaran Cronin (Cambridge: Polity, 2008), pp. 251–70.

17 See my debate with Charles Taylor, *Multiculturalism: Examining the Politics of Recognition* (Princeton, 1994): 'Struggles for Recognition in the Democratic Constitutional State', in J. Habermas, *The Inclusion of the Other*, trans. by Ciaran Cronin (Cambridge: Polity, 1998), pp. 203–36.

18 On the public use of reason, see John Rawls, *Political Liberalism* (New York: Columbia University Press, 1992), pp. 212–54.

19 Ian Buruma, *Murder in Amsterdam: The Death of Theo Van Gogh and the Limits of Tolerance* (New York: Atlantic Books, 2006), p. 34.

20 Timothy Garton Ash, 'Islam in Europe', *New York Review of Books* (5 October 2006).

21 Pascal Bruckner, *signandsight.com*, 24 January 2007: http://www.signandsight.com/features/1146.html (accessed December 2008).

22 'This is the paradox of multiculturalism: it accords the same treatment to all communities, but not to the people who form them, denying them the freedom to liberate themselves from their own traditions' (ibid.). On this, see also Brian Barry, *Culture and Equality* (Cambridge: Polity, 2001); and J. Habermas, 'Equal Treatment of Cultures and the Limits of Postmodern Liberalism, in idem, *Between Naturalism and Religion* (above, n. 16), pp. 271–311.

23 Buruma, *Murder in Amsterdam* (above, n. 19), p. 34.

24 The decisive critique of the incommensurability thesis can be traced back to Donald Davidson's famous 1973 Presidential Address to the American Philosophical Association, 'On the Very Idea of a Conceptual Scheme', in D. Davidson, *Inquiries into Truth and Interpretation* (Oxford: Oxford University Press, 2001), pp. 183–98.

25 Buruma, *Murder in Amsterdam* (above, n. 19), p. 34. Buruma describes the motivation of the Leftist converts as follows (pp. 123f.): 'The Muslims are the spoil-sports who turn up at the party uninvited ... Tolerance has its limits even for the progressivists in Holland. It is easy to be tolerant towards those whom we instinctively think

we can trust, whose jokes we understand and who share our use of irony ... It is far harder to apply this principle to people in our midst who find our way of life as disturbing as we find theirs ...'

26 See my critique in the essays 'Freedom and Determinism', in *Between Naturalism and Religion* (above, n. 16); and 'The Language Game of Responsible Agency and the Problem of Free Will: How Can Epistemic Dualism Be Reconciled with Ontological Monism?', *Philosophical Explorations* 10/1 (2007): 13–50.

27 This is the key issue for John Rawls when he calls for an overlapping consensus between groups with different worldviews on the normative substance of the constitutional order; see J. Rawls, *Political Liberalism* (New York: Columbia University Press, 1993), pp. 133ff.

28 Buruma, 'Tariq Ramadan has an Identity Issue', *New York Times*, 4 February 2007; Bassam Tibi, 'Europeanisation not Islamisation', *signandsight.com*, 22 March 2007: http://www.signandsight.com/features/1258.html (accessed December 2008).

29 On what follows, see Habermas, 'Religion in the Public Sphere', in *Between Naturalism and Religion* (above, n. 16), pp. 114–47.

Chapter 6 European Politics at an Impasse: A Plea for a Policy of Graduated Integration

1 Frank-Walter Steinmeier also professes his faith in the role of utopias in an interview, 'if by "utopia" one means working towards goals that one knows cannot be achieved tomorrow' (*Süddeutsche Zeitung*, 26 October 2007, p. 6). Commitment to goals for the day after tomorrow does not, of course, come cheaply. It set limits to conduct in the present, for example concerning practices we should already refrain from today. When the German government made itself an accomplice of practices of the CIA which violated humanitarian international law, it not only covered up illegal acts but raised doubts concerning the credibility of its most important political aims, namely its commitment to the *imposition* of the primacy of valid

international law over national interests. Cf. Perry Anderson, 'Depicting Europe', *London Review of Books*, 20 September 2007.

2   On the expectations that legal experts associated with the draft constitution, see Armin von Bogdandy, 'Konstitutionalisierung des europäischen öffentlichen Rechts in der europäischen Republik', *Juristenzeitung* 60/11 (2005): 529–40.

3   This is made clear by Joschka Fischer's speech at the Humboldt University Berlin on 12 May 2000, which prompted the discussion concerning a constitutional convention.

4   In Great Britain this agenda is viewed as a matter of course even by the Blair-critical Left, which advocates a 'progressive foreign policy'; see, for example, Charles Grant, 'Europe's Global Role', in David Held and David Mepham (eds), *Progressive Foreign Policy* (Cambridge: Polity, 2007), p. 134: 'Enlargement is in most respects good news for the UK. In a Union of 27 countries, the Franco-German alliance, however resilient it may be, cannot dominate. It is now almost impossible for the UK to become isolated: on tax questions, treaty change, labour market regulation or policy toward some obscure corner of the globe, the UK will almost always find an ally. The old federalist ideology – that in a "political union" the Commission should become an executive government, responsible to both the European Parliament and the Council of Ministers (transformed into an "upper house") – still has adherents in Belgium, Germany, Italy and a few other places. But none of the new members subscribes to this ideology.'

5   Claus Offe (*Die Dynamik der Nachbarschaft*, unpublished ms., June 2007) offers an insightful analysis of the asymmetry between the reasons for accession and its actual consequences. To the economic considerations which spoke in favor of accession on the Polish side corresponded, on the side of the 'old' EU member states, the interest in security and in a reliable neighbor – in addition to normative reasons. Following the accession, by contrast, criticism of the enlargement is growing in the West for economic reasons, but in the East for political,

cultural, and historical reasons. Here the rejection of libertinism and secularism combines with the memory of the national history of suffering into a protest against the curtailment of national sovereignty by 'Brussels'.

6 Andrew Moravcsik, *The Choice for Europe* (Ithaca, NY: Cornell University Press, 1998).

7 Georg Vobruba develops this thesis in *Die Dynamik Europas* (Wiesbaden: VS Verlag, 2005).

8 Ibid., p. 95.

9 Hermann Lübbe, *Abschied vom Superstaat* (Berlin: Siedler, 1994).

10 Erich Rothacker, 'Die deutsche Historische Schule', *Mensch und Geschichte* (Bonn: Bouvier, 1950), pp. 9–20.

11 J. Habermas, 'Does Europe need a constitution?', in idem, *Time of Transitions*, trans. by Ciaran Cronin and Max Pensky (Cambridge: Polity, 2006), pp. 89–109, here at 101ff.

12 See my discussion with Dieter Grimm, who replaced the assertion 'there is no European people' with the more plausible assertion 'there is no European public sphere': Dieter Grimm, *Braucht Europa eine Verfassung?* (Munich: Siemens Stiftung, 1995); J. Habermas, 'Does Europe Need a Constitution? Response to Dieter Grimm', in *The Inclusion of the Other*, trans. by Ciaran Cronin (Cambridge, MA: MIT Press, 1998), pp. 155–61.

13 Bernhard Peters, 'Nationale und transnationale Öffentlichkeit', in idem, *Der Sinn von Öffentlichkeit* (Frankfurt am Main: Suhrkamp, 2007), pp. 283–97.

14 Bernhard Peters, 'Segmentierte Europäisierung: Trends und Muster der Transnationalisierung von Öffentlichkeiten in Europa', in idem, *Der Sinn von Öffentlichkeit* (above, n. 13), pp. 298–321.

15 Granted, the draft constitution did not envisage majority decisions (however qualified) in questions of foreign and security policy either. But here too we must be alert to a difference between 'constitution' and 'treaty' which is not merely 'symbolic'. The political constitution involved the promissory note of an emerging European identity which raised hopes of a circular process involving the promotion of an agreement on questions of foreign policy which would reinforce the sense of solidarity among the

European citizens, while this convergence, in turn, would have promoted common interests in the conduct of foreign policy. Decisions in foreign policy always have a highly symbolic significance for the population concerned, because they touch on existential security needs and on deep-seated mentalities.

16 Jürgen Habermas, *The Postnational Constellation*, trans. by Max Pensky (Cambridge: Polity, 2001).

17 Stephan Leibfried and Michael Zürn (eds), *Transformationen des Staates?* (Frankfurt am Main: Suhrkamp, 2006); Achim Hurrelmann, Stephan Leibfried, Kerstin Martens, and Peter Mayer (eds), *Transforming the Golden-Age Nation State* (Houndmills/Basingstoke: Palgrave Macmillan, 2007).

18 Hauke Brunkhorst, 'Demokratie in der globalen Rechtsgenossenschaft', *Zeitschrift für Soziologie*, Sonderheft Weltgesellschaft (2005), pp. 330–48; Haute Brunkhorst, 'Die Legitimationskrise der Weltgesellschaft: Global Rule of Law, Global Constitutionalism und Weltstaatlichkeit', in Matthias Albert and Rudolf Stichweh (eds), *Weltstaat und Weltstaatlichkeit* (Wiesbaden: VS, 2007), pp. 63–109.

19 On this, see Angelika Emmerich-Fritsche, *Vom Völkerrecht zum Weltrecht* (Berlin: Duncker & Humblot, 2007); Ann Peters, 'Die Zukunft der Völkerrechtswissenschaft: Wider den epistemischen Nationalismus', *Zeitschrift für ausländisches öffentliches Recht und Völkerrecht* 67 (2007): 721–76.

20 Johann P. Arnason, *Civilizations in Dispute* (Leiden: Brill, 2003).

21 The early Carl Schmitt, who defended classical international law and the sovereignty of the subjects of international law against the League of Nations and the prohibition of war, was already a source of inspiration for the founders of the 'realist' school; see Martti Koskenniemi, 'Carl Schmitt, Hans Morgenthau, and the Image of Law in International Relations', in Michael Byers (ed.), *The Role of Law in International Politics* (Oxford: Oxford University Press, 2000), pp. 17–34. Against this, see William E. Scheuerman, 'Revisiting Scientific Man vs Power Politics', *Constellations* 14/4 (2007): 506–30.

22 Even the most powerful enemies are susceptible to black-mail with weapons of mass destruction and acts of terrorism.

23 On what follows, see J. Habermas, 'Does the Constitu-tionalization of International Law Still Have a Chance?', in *The Divided West*, trans. by Ciaran Cronin (Cambridge: Polity, 2006), pp. 115–93; J. Habermas, 'A Political Con-stitution for the Pluralist World Society?', in *Between Naturalism and Religion*, trans. by Ciaran Cronin (Cam-bridge: Polity, 2008), pp. 312–52; J. Habermas, 'Kommu-nikative Rationalität und grenzüberschreitende Politik: eine Replik', in Peter Niesen and Benjamin Herborth (eds), *Anarchie der kommunikativen Freiheit* (Frankfurt am Main: Suhrkamp, 2007), pp. 406–59, here at 452ff.

24 Ngaire Woods, 'Global Economic Governance: A Program for Reform', in Held and Mepham (eds), *Progressive Foreign Policy* (above, n. 4), pp. 213–30.

25 In spite of the objection of the French prime minister, the Lisbon Treaty has not brought much change in this orientation either.

26 Further information on this project can be found under www.tomorrowseurope.eu.

27 Admittedly, there are even some striking voices among their ranks; see for example Andre Brie, 'Die Linke und Europa', *Blätter für deutsche und internationale Politik*, 8 (2007): 985–94. [*Die Linke* (*lit.* 'The Left') is a German left-wing political party formed in 2007 through the merger of the PDS, the successor party of the East German communist party, and the West German WASG, under the joint leadership of Gregor Gysi and former SPD Finance Minister and Chancellor candidate Oscar Lafon-taine. It has made significant electoral gains in recent local and regional elections, mainly at the expense of the SPD. – *Translator's note*]

28 Even the editorial writer of the *Frankfurter Allgemeine Zeitung* (2 January 2008) poses this 'systemic question': 'Many people are only now becoming aware of how much the competition with communism, as long as it persisted, also kept capitalism in check. Democracy and the market economy are no more intrinsically immune to self-destruction than are totalitarian systems. Although, in

contrast to the latter, they have built-in breaks, even the latter are in need of constant inspection and repair.' However, the author, Stefan Dietrich, does not reveal how he understands 'repair' – presumably in more technocratic than democratic terms. He ends the article on a cautionary note, with the warning: 'The elites should pose the systemic question before others do.'

Chapter 7 The Constitutionalization of International Law and the Legitimation Problems of a Constitution for World Society

1 Stephan Leibfried and Michael Zürn (eds), *Transformationen des Staates?* (Frankfurt am Main: Suhrkamp, 2006); Achim Hurrelmann, Stephan Leibfried, Kerstin Martens and Peter Mayer, *Transforming the Golden-Age Nation State* (Hampshire: Palgrave McMillan, 2007).

2 This idea found support primarily among German international lawyers after the Second World War; see, above all, Christian Tomuschat, *International Law: Ensuring the Survival of Mankind*, Collected Courses of the Hague Academy of International Law (1999), Vol. 281 (The Hague: Martinus Nijhoff, 2001); in addition, Jochen A. Frowein, 'Bilanz des 20. Jahrhunderts – Verfassungsrecht und Völkerrecht', in Hartmut Lehmann (ed.), *Rückblicke auf das 20. Jahrhundert* (Göttingen: Wallstein, 2000), pp. 35–54; Bryn-Otto Bryde, 'Konstitutionalisierung des Völkerrechts und Internationalisierung des Verfassungsrechts', *Der Staat* 42 (2003): 62–75. See, more generally, Angelika Emmerich-Fritsche, *Vom Völkerrecht zum Weltrecht* (Berlin: Duncker & Humblot, 2007); Ann Peters, 'Die Zukunft der Völkerrechtswissenschaft: Wider den epistemischen Nationalismus', *Zeitschrift für ausländisches öffentliches Recht und Völkerrecht* 67 (2007): 721–76.

3 Jürgen Habermas, 'The Postnational Constellation and the Future of Democracy', in idem, *The Postnational Constellation: Political Essays*, ed. and trans. by Max Pensky (Cambridge: Polity, 2001), pp. 58–112. By contrast, Daniele Archibugi and David Held (eds), *Cosmopolitan Democracy* (Cambridge: Polity, 1995) and David Held,

Democracy and the Global Order (Cambridge: Polity, 1995) advocate a state model of cosmopolitan democracy; on the idea of a federal world republic, see Otfried Höffe, *Demokratie im Zeitalter der Globalisierung* (Munich: Beck, 1999).

4 Ingeborg Maus, 'Volkssouveränität und das Prinzip der Nichtintervention in der Friedensphilosophie Immanuel Kants', in Hauke Brunkhorst (ed.), *Einmischung erwünscht? Menschenrechte und bewaffnete Intervention* (Frankfurt am Main: Fischer, 1998), pp. 88–116; on the juridification of global politics, see Maus, 'Verfassung oder Vertrag', in Niesen and Herborth (eds), *Anarchie der kommunikativen Freiheit*, pp. 350–82.

5 On the consequences of the failure of the European Constitution, see Habermas, 'European Politics at an Impasse', this volume, pp. 78–105.

6 H. Brunkhorst, 'Demokratie in der globalen Rechts-genossenschaft', *Zeitschrift für Soziologie*, Sonderheft Weltgesellschaft (2005): 330–48; H. Brunkhorst, 'Die Legitimationskrise der Weltgesellschaft: Global Rule of Law, Global Constitutionalism und Weltstaatlichkeit', in Matthias Albert and Rudolf Stichweh (eds), *Weltstaat und Weltstaatlichkeit* (Wiesbaden: VS., 2007), pp. 63–109.

7 J. Habermas, 'A Political Constitution for the Pluralist World Society', in *Between Naturalism and Religion*, trans. by Ciaran Cronin (Cambridge: Polity, 2008), pp. 312–52. [Page numbers in the text refer to this edition.]

8 One can get this impression from the networks of informal legal innovations which, for the most part, escape clear political responsibility and provide the inspiration for the concept of 'global administrative law'. See the symposium on 'Global Governance and Global Administrative Law in the International Legal Order' (Nico Krisch and Benedict Kingsburg, eds) in *European Journal of International Law* 17/1 (February 2006).

9 Rainer Schmalz-Bruns, 'An den Grenzen der Entstaatlichung. Bemerkungen zu Jürgen Habermas' Modell einer "Weltinnenpolitik ohne Weltregierung"', in Niesen and Herborth (eds), *Anarchie der kommunikativen Freiheit* (above, n. 4), pp. 269–93. See also William E. Scheuerman's Review Essay, 'Global Governance without Global

Government? Habermas on Postnational Democracy', *Political Theory* 36/1 (2008): 133–51.

10 Thomas Nagel, 'The Problem of Global Justice', *Philosophy and Public Affairs* 33/2 (2005): 113–47, here at 139ff.

11 Jan-Werner Müller, *Constitutional Patriotism* (Princeton, NJ: Princeton University Press, 2007).

12 This, nevertheless, is the position taken by Joshua Cohen und Charles Sabel in their critique of Nagel's methodological nationalism in 'Extra republicam nulla justistia?', *Philosophy and Public Affairs* 34/2 (2006): 147.

13 Compare the more sceptical account of relevant empirical studies by Patrizia Nanz and Jens Steffek, 'Zivilgesellschaftliche Partizipation und die Demokratisierung internationalen Regierens', in Niesen and Herborth (eds), *Anarchie der kommunikativen Freiheit* (above, n. 4), pp. 87–110.

14 Antje Wiener, 'Demokratischer Konstitutionalismus jenseits des Staates?', in Niesen and Herborth (eds), *Anarchie der kommunikativen Freiheit* (above, n. 4), pp. 173–98.

Chapter 8 Media, Markets and Consumers: The Quality Press as the Backbone of the Political Public Sphere

1 Götz Hamann, 'Kommt die Vierte Gewalt unter den Hammer?', *Die Zeit*, 19 April 2007.

2 Eva C. Schweitzer, 'Erbschleicher von der Wall Street', *Die Zeit*, 26 April 2007.

3 Since then, the Federal Constitutional Court has found in favor of the states in its twelfth judgment on the law regulating broadcasting.

Chapter 9 Political Communication in Media Society: Does Democracy still have an Epistemic Dimension? The Impact of Normative Theory on Empirical Research

1 Elihu Katz, 'Communications Research since Lazarsfeld', *Public Opinion Quarterly* 51 (1989): 25–5: 'Lazarsfeld

and company concluded that it is a good thing for democracy that people can fend off media influence and implied that the crowd may be less lonely and less vulnerable than mass society theorists had led us to believe.' For a critique and metacritique of the 'dominant paradigm', see Todd Gitlin, 'Media Sociology', *Theory and Society* 6 (1978): 205–35; Gaye Tuchman, 'Mass Media Institutions', in Neil J. Smelser (ed.), *Handbook of Sociology* (The Hague: Sage, 1988), pp. 601–26.

2   For example, the critique of Anthony McGann, *The Logic of Democracy* (Ann Arbor: University of Michigan Press, 2006).

3   J. Habermas, 'Three Normative Models of Democracy', in idem, *The Inclusion of the Other*, trans. by Ciaran Cronin (Cambridge, MA: MIT Press, 1998), pp. 239–52.

4   Amy Gutman and Dennis Thompson, *Democracy and Disagreement* (Cambridge, MA: Harvard University Press, 1996); James Bohman, *Public Deliberation* (Cambridge, MA: MIT Press, 1996); Seyla Benhabib, 'Towards a Deliberative Model of Legitimacy', in idem (ed.), *Democracy and Difference* (Princeton: Princeton University Press, 1996), pp. 67–94; James Bohman and William Rehg (eds), *Deliberative Democracy* (Cambridge, MA: MIT Press, 1997).

5   Jürgen Habermas, *Between Facts and Norms*, trans. by William Rehg (Cambridge, MA: MIT Press, 1996).

6   Bernhard Peters, 'Public Discourse, Identity and the Problem of Democratic Legitimacy', in E. O. Erikson (ed.), *Making the European Polity* (London: Routledge, 2005), pp. 84–123.

7   J. Rawls, *Political Liberalism* (New York: Columbia University Press, 1993), pp. 144ff.

8   From this perspective, Bernhard Peters spelled out and tested empirically a theoretical model developed in his postdoctoral thesis, *Die Integration moderner Gesellschaften* (Frankfurt am Main: Suhrkamp, 1993) over the past fifteen years. See, above all, the title essay and 'Die Leistungsfähigkeiten heutiger Öffentlichkeiten – einige theoretische Kontroversen', in B. Peters (ed.), *Der Sinn von Öffentlichkeit* (Frankfurt am Main: Suhrkamp, 2007), pp. 55–102, especially pp. 187–202.

9 Kenneth Arrow, *Social Choice and Individual Values* (New Haven, CT: Yale University Press, 1963).

10 Robert N. Bellah, *The Broken Covenant: American Civil Religion in a Time of Trial* (New York: Seabury Press, 1975); Robert D. Putnam, *Bowling Alone: The Collapse and Revival of American Community* (New York: Simon & Schuster, 2000).

11 Peters, 'Deliberative Öffentlichkeit', in Lutz Wingert and Klaus Günther (eds), *Die Öffentlichkeit der Vernunft und die Vernunft der Öffentlichkeit* (Frankfurt am Main: Suhrkamp, 2001), pp. 655–77.

12 Cristina Lafont, 'Is the Ideal of a Deliberative Democracy Coherent?', in Samantha Besson and Jose Luis Marti (eds), *Deliberative Democracy and its Discontents* (Burlington, VT: Ashgate Publishing, 2006), pp. 3–26.

13 See my reply in *Anarchie der kommunikativen Freiheiten*, edited by Peter Niesen und Benjamin Herborth (Frankfurt am Main: Suhrkamp, 2007), pp. 406–59, here at 413ff.

14 On this, see Bohman and Rehg (eds), *Deliberative Democracy* (above, n. 4).

15 See J. Habermas, 'Some Futher Clarification of the Concept of Communicative Rationality', in idem, *On the Pragmatics of Communication*, trans. Maeve Cook (Cambridge: Polity, 1999), pp. 307–42.; J. Habermas, *Postmetaphysical Thinking*, trans. by William Mark Hohengarten (Cambridge, MA: MIT Press, 1992), pp. 57–112.

16 See J. Habermas, 'Communicative Reason and the Detranscendentalized "Use of Reason"', in *Between Naturalism and Religion*, trans. by Ciaran Cronin (Cambridge: Polity, 2008), pp. 24–76. The normative contents of a 'detranscendentalized reason' embodied in everyday social practices produce a tension within social reality which the sociological observer can subject to rational reconstruction; see Michael A. Neblo, 'Thinking about Democracy: Between the Theory and Practice of Deliberative Politics', *International Journal of Political Science* 40/2 (2005): 169–81. This conception should not be confused with John Rawls's distinction between 'ideal' and 'non-ideal theory'.

17   See Neblo, 'Family Disputes: Diversity in Defining and Measuring Deliberation', *Swiss Political Science Review* 13/4 (2007): 527–57; K. M. Esterling, M. Neblo and D. M. J. Lazer, *Means, Motive, and Opportunity in Becoming Informed about Politics: A Deliberative Field Experiment* (PNG Working paper No. PNG07–006, available online at: http://www.hks.harvard.edu/netgov/files/png_ workingpaper_series/PNG07–006.pdf (accessed August 2008).

18   M. Neblo, 'Change for the Better? Linking the Mechanisms of Deliberative Opinion Change to Normative Theory', in idem, *Common Voices: The Problems and Promise of a Deliberative Democracy* (forthcoming), available online at: http://polisci.osu.edu/faculty/mneblo/ papers/ChangeC4.pdf (accessed August 2008).

19   James S. Fishkin, *The Voice of the People: Public Opinion and Democracy* (New Haven, CT: Yale University Press, 1995); Fishkin and Robert C. Luskin, 'Experimenting with a democratic Ideal: Deliberative Polling and Public Opinion', *Acta Politica* 40 (September 2005), pp. 284–98.

20   Andre Blais, R. Kenneth Carty, and Patrick Fournier, *Do Citizen Assemblies Make Reasonable Choices?* (forthcoming).

21   James Johnson, 'Is Talk Really Cheap? Prompting Conversation between Critical Theory and Rational Choice', *American Political Review* 87 (1993): 74–86; Joseph Heath, *Communicative Action and Rational Choice* (Cambridge, MA: MIT Press, 2001).

22   James N. Druckman, 'Political Preference Formation: Competition, Deliberation and the (Ir)Relevance of Framing Effects', *American Political Science Review* 98 (2004): 671–86, here at 675: 'Individuals who engage in conversations with a heterogeneous group will be less susceptible to framing effects than those who do not engage in conversations.'

23   Bruce E. Gronbeck, 'Rhetoric and Politics', in Lynda Lee Kaid (ed.), *Handbook of Political Communication Research* (Mahwa, NJ: Lawrence Erlbaum Associates, 2004), pp. 135–54.

24   Wolfgang van den Daele, *Technikfolgenabschätzung als politisches Argument* (Berlin: Wissenschaftszentrum

Berlin, 1994); W. van den Daele, 'Objektives Wissen als politische Ressource: Experten und Gegenexperten im Diskus', in W. van den Daele and Friedhelm Neidhardt (eds), *Kommunikation und Entscheidung: WZB-Jahrbuch 1996* (Berlin: Sigma, 1996), pp. 297–326; W. van den Daele, Rainer Döbert, and Achim Seiler, 'Stakeholder Dialogue on Intellectual Property Rights in Biotechnology: A Project of the World Business Council for Sustainable Development', *International Review of Industrial Property and Copyright Law* 34/8 (2003): 932–52.

25 W. Van den Daele and Neidhardt, 'Regierung durch Diskussion - über Versuche, mit Argumenten Politik zu machen', in W. van den Daele and Neidhardt (eds), *Kommunikation und Entscheidung* (above, n. 24), pp. 9–50.

26 Alistair S. Duff, 'Daniel Bell's Theory of the Information Society', *Journal of Information Science* 24 (1998): 373–93.

27 For the quantification and measurement of societal information flows, see A. S. Duff and Joho Shakai, 'The Japanese Contribution to Information Society Studies', *Keio Communication review* 22 (2000): 41–77.

28 For the 'digital divide' between Internet users and non-users, see Simon R. B. Berdal, *Public Deliberation on the Web: A Habermasian Inquiry Into Online Discourse*, Hovedfag Thesis (Oslo: University of Oslo/Department of Informatics, August 2004), pp. 51–6; available online under: http://heim.ifi.uio.no/~simonb/Studier/hfag/FERDIG/CD/thesis.pdf (accessed August 2008).

29 Manuel Castells, *The Rise of the Network Society*, Vol. 1 (Oxford: Blackwell, 1996).

30 Habermas, *Between Facts and Norms* (above, n. 5), pp. 359–87.

31 I am following the main lines of Bernhard Peters' analysis in 'Über öffentliche Deliberation und öffentliche Kultur' from 1997, reprinted in Peters, *Der Sinn von Öffentlichkeit* (above, n. 8), pp. 103–86.

32 Van den Daele, 'Objektives Wissen als politische Ressource' (above, n. 24), pp.18f.

33 On the connection between online communication and the public sphere, see Christoph Bieber, *Politische Projekte im Internet* (Frankfurt am Main/New York: Campus, 1999); see also the contributions in Section 3 of Andrew

Feenberg und Darin Barney (eds), *Community in the Digital Age* (Lanham, MD: Rowman & Littlefield, 2004), pp. 183ff. For a comparative analysis of the organization and infrastructure of web fora linked to *Der Spiegel* (Germany), *The Guardian* (UK), and *Aftenposten* (Sweden), respectively, see Berdal, *Public Deliberation on the Web* (above, n. 28).

34 An indicator for the critical function of such a parasitical form of online communication is the bill for €2,088, which the moderator of Bildblog.de recently sent to the commissioning editor of Bild.de for 'services'. The bloggers claimed that they had improved the work of the editorial staff of the *Bild-Zeitung* (Germany's largest-selling tabloid newspaper) with useful criticisms and corrections. See the article 'Medienwächter als Dienstleister', which appeared on 2 May 2006 in the online edition of *Süddeutschen Zeitung*; available at: http://www.sueddeutsche.de/computer/artikel/898/74824/ (accessed August 2008).

35 Jürg Steiner, Andre Bächtiger, Markus Spörndli, and Marco R. Steenbergen, *Deliberative Politics in Action* (Cambridge: Cambridge University Press, 2004); see also my reflections on this issue in the essay 'Concluding Comments on Empirical Approaches to Deliberative Politics', *Acta Politica* 40/3 (2005): 384–92, here at 389f.

36 Pamela Johnston Canover and Donald D. Searing, 'Studying "Everyday Talk" in the Deliberative System', *Acta Politica* 40/3 (2005): pp. 269–83.

37 Simone Chambers, 'Measuring Publicity's Effect: Reconciling Empirical Research and Normative Theory', *Acta Politica* 40/3 (2005): 255–66.

38 Katharina Holzinger, 'Context or Conflict Types: Which Determines the Selection of Communication Mode?', *Acta Politica* 40/3 (2005): 239–54.

39 Peters, *Der Sinn von Öffentlichkeit* (above, n. 8), pp. 76ff. and 145ff.

40 J. Gerhards, *Neue Konfliktlinien in der Mobilisierung öffentlicher Meinung* (Opladen: Leske + Budrich, 1993), p. 26.

41 Otfried Jarren and Patrick Donges, *Politische Kommunikation in der Mediengesellschaft* (Wiesbaden: VS., 2006), pp. 119ff. and 329ff.

217

42 Karen Callaghan and Frauke Schnell, *Framing American Politics* (Pittsburgh: University of Pittsburgh Press, 2005), pp. 1–20.

43 Jarren and Donges, *Politische Kommunikation in der Mediengesellschaft* (above, n. 41), pp. 26ff.; Bernd Weisbrod, 'Öffentlichkeit als politischer Prozess. Dimensionen der politischen Medialisierung in der Geschichte der Bundesrepublik', in idem (ed.), *Die Politik der Öffentlichkeit – Die Öffentlichkeit der Politik. Politische Medialisierung in der Geschichte der Bundesrepublik* (Göttingen: Wallstein, 2003), pp. 11–28.

44 John B. Thompson, *The Media and Modernity* (Cambridge: Polity, 1995), pp. 258ff.

45 Russell J. Dalton, *Citizen Politics: Public Opinion and Political Parties in Advanced Industrial Democracies* (Washington: CQ Press, 2006), p. 22.

46 Jarren and Donges, *Politische Kommunikation in der Mediengesellschaft* (above, n. 41), pp. 180–95.

47 'At the moment of publication they lose control over the issue and its interpretations; for even when an issue is adopted entirely, the reaction to it and the attendant communication are not predictable' (ibid., p. 360).

48 Ilya Somin, 'Voter Ignorance and the Democratic Ideal', *Critical Review* 12 (1998): 413–58; Matthew Weinshall, 'Means, Ends, and Public Ignorance in Habermas' Theory of Democracy', *Critical Review* 15 (2003): 23–58; Jeffrey Friedman, 'Public Opinion: Bringing the Media Back', *Critical Review* 15 (2003): 239–60.

49 Robert B. Talisse, 'Does Public Ignorance Defeat Deliberative Democracy?' *Critical Review* 16 (2004): 455–64.

50 Michael X. Delli Carpini, 'Mediating Democratic Engagement: The Impact of Communications on Citizens' Involvement in Political and Civic Life', in Kaid (ed.), *Handbook of Political Communication Research* (above, n. 23), pp. 395–434, here at 412; Dalton, *Citizen Politics* (above, n. 45), pp. 26ff.

51 In the context of the present discussion of communication studies, I cannot address the further requirement that the public sphere must ensure the transparency of all relevant policy-making and decision-making processes. This requires that all political demands raised by appeal

to the functional imperatives of the economic systems must be channeled through the public sphere. This touches on the long-standing controversy over democracy and capitalism; cf. Claus Offe, *Strukturprobleme des kapitalistischen Staates*, rev. edn (Frankfurt am Main/New York: Campus, 2005).

52 Cinzia Padovani, *A Fatal Attraction: Public Television and Politics in Italy* (Lanham, MD: Rowman & Littlefield, 2005), pp. 1–12.

53 Robert M. Entman, *Projections of Power* (Chicago: Chicago University Press, 2004), pp. 1–22.

54 Lee Artz and Y. R. Kamalipour (eds), *Bring 'em On: Media and Politics in the Iraq War* (Lanham, MD: Rowman & Littlefield, 2005).

55 Paul Ginsborg, *Silvio Berlusconi. Television, Power and Patrimony* (London: Verso, 2004), p. 40.

56 Sidney Verba, Kay Lehman Schlozman, and Henry Brady, *Voice and Equality: Civic Voluntarism in American Politics* (Cambridge, MA: Harvard University Press, 1995); Delli Carpini, 'Mediating Democratic Engagement' (above, n. 50), pp. 404ff.

57 Michael Vester, Peter von Oertzen, Heiko Geiling, Thomas Hermann, and Dagmar Müller, *Soziale Milieus im gesellschaftlichen Strukturwandel* (Frankfurt am Main: Suhrkamp, 2001).

58 Dalton, *Citizen Politics* (above, n. 45), pp. 172ff., 219ff.

59 Ibid., pp. 121f., 206ff.

60 Delli Carpini, 'Mediating Democratic Engagement' (above, n. 50), pp. 420ff.

61 Tsieng-Tsung Lee, 'Media Effects on Political Disengagement Revisited', *Journalism and Mass Communication Quarterly* 82 (2005): 416–33, here at 421ff.

62 Carl Boggs, 'The Great Retreat: Decline of the Public Sphere in Late Twentieth-Century America', *Theory and Society* 26 (1997): 741–80.

63 'Candidates' images can be seen as commodities packaged by image makers who sway the public by emphasizing traits with special appeal to voters.' Dalton, *Citizen Politics* (above, n. 45), p. 215.

64 Jarren and Donges, *Politische Kommunikation in der Mediengesellschaft* (above, n. 41), pp. 163, 384ff.

219

65 Knut Hickethier, 'Der politische Blick im Dispositiv Fernsehen', in Weisbrod (ed.), *Die Politik der Öffentlichkeit* (above, n. 43), pp. 79–96.

66 See for example the interesting studies of Tasuro Hunada, such as 'Can There Be a Public Sphere in Japan?', *Review of Media, Information and Society* 2 (1997): 1–23, or 'Towards a Politics of the Public Sphere', *Review of Media, Information and Society* 4 (1999): 115–33.

67 Achim Hurrelmann, Stephan Leibfried, Kerstin Martens, and Peter Mayer (eds), *Transforming the Golden-Age Nation State* (Houndmills/Basingstoke: Palgrave Macmillan, 2007).

68 Patrizia Nanz and Jens Steffek, 'Zivilgesellschaftliche Partizipation und die Demokratisierung internationalen Regierens', in Niesen and Herborth (eds), *Anarchie der kommunikativen Freiheiten* (above, n. 13), pp. 87–110.

69 This is why the Lisbon Treaty sets the national parliaments a deadline for a deferred veto.

70 J. Habermas, 'Does Europe Need a Constitution?', in idem, *Time of Transitions*, trans. by Ciaran Cronin and Max Pensky (Cambridge: Polity, 2006), pp. 89–109, here at 101ff.

71 Bernhard Peters describes this process as the step (a) from the observation of European issues in one's own national public sphere (b) to the reciprocal observation of the national publics with respect to these issues and (c) to the discursive exchange between the national publics on these issues; with this (d) he associates the prospect of the communicative production of a collective identity. On this see Peters, *Der Sinn von Öffentlichkeit* (above, n. 8), pp. 298ff.

Index